Serenity They Seek

by

Vanessa L. Greer

The contents of this work including, but not limited to, the accuracy of events, people, and places depicted; opinions expressed; permission to use previously published materials included; and any advice given or actions advocated are solely the responsibility of the author, who assumes all liability for said work and indemnifies the publisher against any claims stemming frompublication of the work.

All Rights Reserved
Copyright © 2021 by Vanessa L. Greer
No part of this book may be reproduced or transmitted
in any form or by any means, electronic or mechanical,
including photocopying, recording, or by any information
storage and retrieval system without permission in
writing from the author.
ISBN: 978-1-956419-00-9
eISBN: 978-1-956419-01-6
Printed in the United States of America
Second Printing

Serenity They Seek

On her way to work, Valoria decided to stop by the grocery store around the corner from her office to pick up some fruits for her snack for the day. As she approached the checkout line, she noticed that the line was not moving. "Do they only have one cashier?" she asked the impatient customer in front of her, who continuously huffed and puffed. She finally looked a few customers ahead to see what the holdup was. There was a lady at the register, slowly putting back items least important on her grocery list so she could balance the register to what was in her pocket. The woman had one small child and two older kids. They were quiet and watched as their mother put back things on her list. Val was not rich, but she was more fortunate than the woman. Everyone else in the line watched and waited impatiently as she rummaged around her grocery basket. Val stared and thought about when she and Isaac would come to the grocery store, how he picked up at least five items he wanted, but were not needed. Val, then, instantly had compassion in her heart. She went to the beginning of the line and told the woman to keep everything she was putting back, and that she would cover the cost. The lady looked at her with amazement, smiled, and thanked her deeply. The woman's two older children looked at Val and beamed. After paying the cashier for the remainder of the woman's groceries, Val made her way back to the end of the line. She noticed that there was an old woman staring from the aisle where the line ended. Val smiled at the old woman and turned to face the line as it proceeded to move.

"Good morning, Charity. Do I have any messages?" Val said.

"Yes, Ma'am, two of your clients called and asked to be rescheduled for next week," Charity replied.

"Thanks, could you please forward me my agenda for the day?" Val asked.

"Yes, Ma'am," Charity responded.

"Charity, can I ask you something?"

"Ask away."

"Is everything going good with you? You just seem to be a little bit more excited than usual."

"Ha-ha-ha, now, Val, why would you think something is wrong with me? Is it because I am so happy lately? Val, you are analyzing everything. I think you need a vacation."

"Ha-ha-ha, maybe you are right," agreed Val. "Well, I hope you are ready to make this day happen with me." She walked off and entered her office to prepare for her busy and productive day.

"I wonder if she really thinks something is wrong with me. I hope she doesn't ask me again. I really don't think I can keep a straight face next time," Charity wondered out loud.

"I have so much to do before my day starts, but before I start my day, I need some extra strength and guidance," Val said, and then prayed, "Lord, I want to thank you for waking me up this morning and allowing me to be able to see the beauty of daylight once again. I want to thank you for blessing me with the strength and the knowledge of guidance for today. Lord is with me, Amen!

"Let's see who I have for today. Hum, Antwan, I have never heard that name before, but I do recognize Charlene. I haven't heard from her in a while." The phone rang. "This is Valoria, how can I help you?"

A man's voice replied, really soft and trembly, saying, "Val, when my son comes in today, please try to help him. I have been having bad feelings about him and his situation."

"Okay, but if you don't mind, can you please tell me who you are? I don't recognize your voice," Val replied.

"It's me, Allen. I have needed to talk to you all weekend. It's my son, Antwan."

Val remembered the name on her agenda for the day. "Okay, Mr. Allen, you don't have to go into full detail of what's going on. I'll talk to him when he gets here at 10:30 A.M. Thanks for calling. I'll be looking out for him, but because of confidentiality, I will not be able to discuss what we have talked about."

"I don't care about that, Val. I just need for you to try to reach him. Please, Val, he won't listen. What have I done?"

"Mr. Allen, do not blame yourself for your son's actions or attitude. He is an adult, right?"

"Yes."

"Every child is raised, whether it is good or bad, but somewhere down the road in life, he or she is exposed to correct decision making. Don't worry about him right now. He will be here shortly, so go ahead and get yourself together and never forget what I told you."

"Thanks, Val!"

"Always," Val replied then hung up. Shortly after she put the phone down, there was a knock on the door. "It's open!" Val shouted. In walked the old woman whom Val had seen in the grocery store earlier. Val stood up, as if she had seen a ghost. "Well, hello! How may I help you?" The old woman just stood there with a distant look on her face. She looked as if she was trying to figure out a question in her head. She had on very old-fashioned clothes, but what was very odd was that her handbag was very modern. Val assumed that, maybe, she got the bag as a gift from someone who might have been close to her. She asked once again, but this time, much more excited and softer, with a warm and welcoming smile. "How may I help you?" The old lady just looked at her and did not say a word. "Would you like to have a seat?"

The woman then promptly said, "I'm sorry for bothering you." She turned and walked back out the door.

Val then called Charity, "Charity?"

"Val, I already know what you are going to ask me. The old lady came in and was looking around as if she was looking for something, and then, she asked me, 'Did the lady with the green sweater and black pants come in here?' I asked her, 'Are you talking about Val?' She did not respond. She just looked at me, funny. She was very weird! I then proceeded to tell her that, 'yes, Val does have on a green sweater and black pants. I told her this was your office. She then just headed directly to your door. Your 10:30 appointment was here, sitting in the lobby. I have never seen him before, so I didn't want to scare him off by letting it be known that a weird woman was walking into your office. I did, in fact, stand by the door with my cordless phone in one hand with 911 on redial and my mace in the other. Who is she? And what did she want?"

"I'm not sure," Val replied. "She did not say anything. She just gave me a distant look. But what really puzzles me is that I saw her in the grocery store this morning, when I stopped by to get some oranges. I think she followed me, Charity!"

"Followed you?" Charity asked, confused.

"How else would she know where to find me? Why would she come in, turn around, and walk out? I'm puzzled."

"There you go, dissecting and analyzing everything again," said Charity.

"Ha-ha-ha-ha, you know that you were just as much shocked as I was," remarked Val.

"Ha-ha-ha-ha, you are right about that. Are you ready for you first appointment?"

"Sure, send him in."

"She will see you now, Mr. Antwan, but before you go in, can I get you to sign one more form for me?" Charity told Antwan.

"Yeah," Antwan replied.

After Antwan signed the form, he proceeded to walk into Val's office. When the doorknob turned, Val instantly swallowed deep and stood beside her desk, waiting to greet the new client. As Antwan entered the room, Val proceeded to walk close to him to properly introduce herself. "Hello, Antwan, I'm Val. Your father called me and told me to expect you."

His voice was very smooth and deep as he responded, "What's up? I mean, hello." He looked as if he had been up all night long. He resembled his father, Allen, very much. He was just a tad bit lighter than Allen, and just a little bit taller. His clothes were very sporty, and he was very well groomed.

"Have a seat. Talk to me, Antwan. Tell me a little about you," Val said.

"Well, there is not much I can tell other than my dad is so worried about me. He promised if I would go see a shrink, he would leave me alone for life, so, I agreed. Look, there is not very much for me to tell that I would want to volunteer to because really, I don't know you. You could be a cop posing to be a shrink to get dirt and information on people's lives," Antwan replied. He laughed and said, "Ha-ha, you know what? Why don't you tell me something about yourself? It's funny that all you do is sit around, asking people questions, but no one asks you questions, so please, allow me to be the first to ask you, or do I need to pay you first?"

"What would make you think that I want you to pay me anything?" asked Val.

"Come on now, you know, as well as I do, nothing in this life is free. Everybody knows that shrinks get paid lots of money to sit around and try to figure people out. You know what? This is a waste of my time. I have kept my promise. I have stepped into your office, and now, I'm about to step out. Good day!" As he started out of the door, all Val could do was watch him walk away. She said nothing to him because she knew that, somehow, he would find out that everything he said about her was, in fact, his theory.

As Antwan walked past Charity's desk, he turned and asked her, "What was that last form that you had me to sign?"

"That form just simply states that we are a nonprofit organization and that we do not charge for any services rendered. It also states that you understand that we work solely off donations and gift contributions," Charity answered. The look on his face was that of a man who had just been sentenced to a life term in prison. "Would you like to schedule for another session?" Charity asked. Antwan looked at her with disgust. He then turned and looked at Val's door and walked off.

Val just sat down at her desk and typed on her laptop about what had just happened. Suddenly, her phone rang. She answered, "This is Valoria. How may I help you?" There was complete silence on the line. After repeating herself three times, Val just hung up.

A few hours had passed. Charity knocked on the door before entering. "Hey, Val, are you ready for Charlene? She is about thirty minutes early," Charity said.

"Sure, send her in," Val replied.

"Good afternoon, Charlene. How have you been? I haven't heard from you in a while. I'll assume that is a good thing," Val greeted.

"Hey, Val! I just needed someone whom I could talk to, someone I know I could trust," Charlene responded.

"Well, you came to the right person. What's going on?"

"Well, Val, I took your advice the last time I talked to you, and so far, everything has been going okay for the most part, but I still have this problem that I just can't seem to shake."

"And what's that?"

"I feel like I hate men, and really, I don't think I will ever trust anyone ever again as long as I live," replied Charlene. "Last week, when I went to this convention with my job, I met this top executive. He is a very nice-looking guy, with a very high drive for success, but the only problem is, I noticed him first and kind of gave him a flirty smile, but not really wanting him to respond. He was halfway across the room. He immediately stopped talking to the people he was talking to and approached me. He came over and said, 'I haven't seen you here before, Charlene.' I was shocked, not knowing how he knew my name, but I then realized that I was wearing a name tag. He asked me about the company that I worked for, and then after he asked me to go out for dinner later that night."

"What did you say?"

"I told him no, but he could call me. I really don't know why I told him that because he has been calling me every day since I gave him my number."

"Is that not what you wanted?" inquired Val.

"At first, I thought I did, but after talking to him, I find myself being extremely mean and sometimes making really smart remarks that are very critical."

"Why do you feel like you have to say the things you say to him?"

"I don't know," Charlene said. "I feel like just because he has money, it does not mean anything. I feel like the ones with money are worse dogs than the ones without it. He acts like it does not bother him that I'm like that. He acts as if he really understands."

"Has he made any attempt to want to see you or insinuate that he is serious about getting to know you other than talking to you on the phone?"

"No, he just calls to see how I am doing and talks about things that I am not even interested in hearing about."

"And what's that?"

"Sports, business, his travel plans, and his past relationships."

"So, since you seem to know what you want to hear, please share with me what type of things do you want to hear?" Val was curious.

"Uhhh, I don't know just anything other than what he wants to talk about. I don't know, Val. I guess I am just crazy."

"No, you are not crazy," Val replied calmly. "You just don't want to make a mistake and get involved with someone who will hurt you in the future. You see, I can understand why you feel that way, but what I can't understand is why you don't know what exactly you want to hear. Give me a minute while I try to understand the concept of your feelings. There are some things you have to take into consideration. The conversation that you may find boring may be what's important in his life at this time. How do you know if he really understands or not? Men and women are two different species, but we are all the same. When God created a woman from man, we inherited the softer side of him. Because we are not full man, there is so much strength that we have. We can be strong like men and sometimes stronger emotionally and socially, but our physical strength is limited. Now, our physical lifestyle affects the way we feel emotionally. When a woman gets physically hurt so many times, there is only so much she allows herself to go through again. Since she is a woman and has a much softer side, her forgiveness level is high, because of whom she is, a woman. A man, on the other hand, has very little tolerance for pain. Because we have taken a large portion of his sensitivity, he uses his physical strength to help him get through an emotional situation, such as finding something to do physically to completely take his mind off what's happening. I'm not saying that men don't have a sensitive side and don't forgive. I'm just saying they don't break down the way we do. Men do cry and they do have feelings, but most of them would much rather be single and play the field. This will keep him from experiencing the heartbreak marathon. We, as women, always want someone. I don't care how badly or how many times we have been hurt. We long to have that one true love that will give us the love and happiness that we feel we deserve. I think I know what kind of conversation you are looking for, and I might be wrong, given that only God knows where your heart is. I am going to take your explanation and weigh it to this. The conversation you want to hear is: what kind of woman he is looking for and had prayed for. You want to hear that everything is going to be okay. It would be nice for him to tell you that it is okay for you to trust again one day, since you cannot interfere with what is meant to be. You want to hear him tell the story of how he wants to make his woman happy because that is what she would deserve.

"Every woman is a mother of this world, no matter how old or young she is. Somehow, if it is in God's will, she will bear the fruit of the nation. The man has the seed, but the woman has the nourishment and love that it needs to grow inside and outside the womb. Charlene, you are not the only woman who has trust issues when it comes to men and relationships. There are so many women who feel broken and deserted, as if life has stopped in their path. Many have lots of children, many have war scars, many have habits and addictions, many have weight problems, many have turned to themselves for the sensitive touch, and many feel they are not attractive enough to be loved. Every woman I just named is a nourishment of this nation. The man is responsible or making sure that the crop is well harvested and planted in the right ground. If he plants a seed and it grows into nourishment, it is up to him to make sure that the nourishment can continue to the end. If he helps destroy it, it will, in fact, one day destroy him and all the harvesters to come. Charlene, even though you feel as if you will never trust again, you have to remember that not every man is out here to tear down who you are. There are so many men who are just like you. They don't trust. A man fears of being the best for a woman, who may hurt him because of her past, even though he is not the one who hurt her. I'm not saying you have to take a risk on every man you meet, but I am saying you need to open your mind and let God send you your husband, if it is in his will."

"What if I open my mind, but it is not in his will?" Charlene questioned.

"That is something you and I will never know, so that's why you must open up your mind and give no one, but God, your heart. He will then give you the desires of it, but you have to have faith, and if it is something your heart truly desires, only God will know."

"So, should I continue to talk to this man on the phone and listen to what I don't want to hear?"

"Only if you want to," said Val patiently. "Listen to him talk one more time, and if you notice that you are not the main topic of his conversation, then let him know nicely that you are not interested. If you are truly someone, he seeks, then his persistence will show you that he is truly seeking for an answer to his prayer."

"How would I know if he is a man who prays by his persistence?" Charlene asked. "He could be trying to be persistent to try to get me in his bedroom."

"That is a lustful persistence that you will recognize. This persistence will be different. It will be a persistence you never knew before. It will be without lust, money, or deceit. It will be a persistence that can only come from above.

"Charlene, you are a very successful woman, and your past has not been the easiest thing to try to overcome. All you want to be is happy, but I always want you to remember to always seek God first, and the rest will soon follow."

"Thanks, Val. For one so young, your advice is always wise."

"I would like to think that everyone who walks through my door would receive a kind word from me," said Val.

"So, as I am leaving, I will stop by Charity and have her schedule me for one day next week. There's something else I want to talk to you about, but I have said enough for one day, and I need to relax my mind. I'll see you next week," Charlene said.

As Charlene left, Val followed her out of the office to Charity's desk. "Charity, could you please put Charlene on the schedule for next week. We have only one hour left to go. I think I will finish up my day by doing some online shopping. Do you want to join the coolest boss in America?" Val told Charity.

"Sure, as soon as I am done calling your four clients for tomorrow," Charity responded.

"Four?" Val asked. "That's fine. I'll already be halfway done by the time you get done. I'll be sure and buy you something. Ha-ha!"

The next morning, Val was headed to the office and decided she wanted a fresh pineapple, but this time, she was headed to the store a few blocks away from the store she went to yesterday to get her oranges. She was hoping she would not run into the little old lady whom she had seen at that grocery store. She was not afraid or anything, but it just seemed a little weird for her to see her at the store then an hour or so later, she ended up in her office just staring.

On her way back to the produce section, a surprise was waiting for her. It was a person whom she had seen once before in the past, when she was the old Val. She had since then changed her life around and lived for the truth, for God. His name was Zack. She had seen him around from time to time, but she never met him. She knew of his name through people she associated with. He was brown-skinned, with a body of a football player. He was slightly tall, well groomed, and had a smile that would make any woman melt. As she approached the fruit section, he, dressed in a business suit, was walking in her direction. As she was looking through the fruit, he stopped next to her and was looking at the grapefruit next to the pineapple.

"Nice morning to enjoy a bowl of fruit for breakfast?" Zack asked.

"Sure is," Val said without looking.

"Hey, I have seen you somewhere before."

"Really?" replied Val. "I have seen you somewhere before, too, but it has been a while since I have seen you."

"Oh really? Where do you think you have seen me? And how long ago was it?" Zack pried.

"Oh, around town, and I would say it has been about six years since I had last seen you," Val said.

"I'm glad you remember—because I don't. All I know is that I have seen you before. Ha-ha-ha-ha," said Zack. "What is your name?"

"Valoria."

"Nice to meet you, Valoria. My name is Zack. Are you headed to work?"

"Yes, Sir."

"You are not very talkative, are you?"

"More than you know."

"If you don't mind me complimenting you, but you look very appealing this morning. What type of work do you do?"

"I am a counselor," Val answered.

"A shrink, huh?"

"Call it what you may."

"I'm sorry. That is just what I have always known for it to be. So, if I needed to come and see you for a problem I'm having, how much would you charge me?"

"My services are free."

"Free! How do you have an office if you don't have income to pay for your space?" Zack asked, surprised.

"God has provided a way for me to run a business without charging people to get the help they need. You see, Zack, not everything you need in life has a price to follow. I'm able to pay my bills and employees from donations and gift contributions," Val explained.

"That is great! I have never heard of a free shrink."

"Well, that goes to show that just because you have not seen or heard of it before does not mean it does not exist."

"You are so right. So, knowing that, is it possible for me to come and see you? I really would like to have someone to talk to about my problems, but I would first like to know what I would be dealing with."

"Sure," Val answered, then handed him one of her business cards. "Well, Zack, it was nice to see you again, but I really must run, I have some appointments that I need to make."

"When can I call for an appointment?"

"Anytime at your convenience. See ya!" Val left.

Val arrived at her office. "Good morning, Val," Charity greeted.

"Good morning, smiley face. You know, Charity, I really love this new you. I'm starting to think that the Lord has answered my prayer. When you first started, I was a little worried if I was going to be able to deal with you, but it set so well with my spirit to give you the job, with your attitude and all," Val responded. "Do I have any messages?"

"No, unfortunately, not this morning, and that really puzzles me because normally, Tuesdays are my phone days because everyone knows the busiest day has come and gone, but you do have three appointments. Two are walk-ins: Jermaine, your regular, and Tamya and Charles."

"Okay, thanks, I'll get prepared for my day." When Val walked in her office, she felt a little uneasy, as if she knew that today was going to be a challenge. So, the first thing she did was go to her chair, got on her knees, and began to pray. "Lord, I need you to speak directly through me today. I have a feeling that the issues that will be brought forth to me today are going to be issues that my advice and kind words cannot even touch. Lord, thank you for already blessing my tongue. I love you, Lord, and thank you for always ordering my steps."

"Val?" Charity called.

"Yes?" Val answered.

"Your first walk-in has arrived."

"Okay, send the person in."

In walked Tamya. She was a very shy woman who had a quiet personality. She had on a toboggan with an outfit to match. "Hello!" Val greeted.

"Hello," Tamya replied.

"Have a seat. My name is Valoria, but you are welcome to call me Val for short. Would you like something to drink?"

"No, Ma'am, I just came because I needed someone to talk to. Someone told me about you, and they told me that your services are free. Look, I'm not coming here because I'm crazy or needs medication. I just need someone to listen to me without judging me," Tamya said.

"Well, you certainly came to the right place," said Val. "What can I help you with?"

"Well, I have this habit I seem to can't quit. I have tried everything possible, but I just can't shake it because of the stress in my life. Sometimes, I get so mad that I want to kill someone, or better yet, go and kill everyone who has ever caused me to hurt in my life—that even includes old boyfriends, one-night stands, and childhood bullies." All of a sudden, Tamya began crying and yelling hysterically.

"Please, just breathe," Val yelled over the screaming. Tamya continued to scream and cry louder and louder. Val instantly fell to the floor to her knees and prayed silently, "Lord, now you must take this visit for me, now please, Lord!"

Tamya calmed down and looked at Valoria, then she said, "What are you doing?"

Valoria did not hear her because she was receiving the spirit that would speak through her. Val looked at the woman and noticed she was staring at her with a look that could not be explained. "Tamya, have you ever prayed before?" Val asked.

"Yes, but that does not work."

"If you don't mind me asking, what is this habit that you cannot break?"

"I have a cocaine and weed addiction," replied Tamya. "There's more to it than you think. I have turned into a pure junky. If I don't have one of those drugs, I snap. I have quit jobs because I could not get it as quick as I needed it. Because of it, my three kids have suffered. When I am in-between jobs like that, they are never able to get anything because I am constantly playing catchup. I have two fathers for my three kids. My youngest has her own father, but he left. My other two girls have begun to cry every night because they feel sorry for their baby sister. Her father is not in her life, and she has not had a new pair of shoes in four months, so she has to wear her older sister's shoes that are too big. I know you probably think I'm spending my money on the drugs, but that's not the case. I never pay for them. The guys I have sex with always have something for me to do."

"I see," said Val. "Everything that you are going through sounds as if it's a pattern that has turned into a lifestyle. Where are the fathers? Do they give you any help at all?

"The father of my first and second child is in prison, while my youngest child's father had four other kids after her, and he does not work. I have not heard from him in about eight months."

"I see. If you don't mind, I would like to tell you a story that is a whole lot similar to yours," Val said to her patient. "She is a woman who thought her life was not worth living. She used to smoke weed and snort cocaine every chance she got. With doing that, her anger grew enormously. She began to hate everyone around her. She wanted everyone who had ever hurt her to feel the pain, but worse than they had inflicted on her. One day, she cried so hard that she threw up, and when she threw up, her mind began to race with negative and positive thoughts, but the positive thoughts outweighed the negative, so she began to let them play. I will give you the order of the negative and draw a line to what good came out of it. Let's start with the cocaine and weed. When she smoked or snorted cocaine, her stress went numb. She was unable to be stressed, but her mind continued to race. In fact, she was almost in a more clear-thought realm. But because she was free of stress, she found herself making spur-of-the-moment decisions such as sleeping with men who did not care about her. She also found herself in a neglectful state of mind. Everything good around seemed to look like a fairytale, so she treated it as such. All of those habits began to reveal their harmful intentions, as she noticed everything she had worked hard for began to fade slowly, as if someone was trying to get her attention. She became angry because there was no proof of why she was losing things, so she began to blame everyone who had a bad part in her past, to try to cover up and not think about what was really happening. So, eventually, as time went by, she had gotten rid of everyone. No one wanted to have anything to do with her because she had become so bitter. The strangest thing happened after everything and everybody was gone. She no longer had an excuse, a habit, or no one to blame—all of a sudden, she began to breathe. When she started to breathe, things started happening. She, without knowing, had weeded out everything that was harmful to her mind, body, and soul. Her mind had even taken a drastic turn. Her way of thinking became more positive. She eventually got back everything she had lost, and in the process, met a whole new team of friends, who had all approached her with positiveness and love. She had no idea why all of a sudden everything began to look good, until she met this one lady, who took to her like a big sister, and through all of her almost relapse of a bad lifestyle, she spoke nothing but greatness about her. This lady eventually faded out of her life. She was almost discouraged by this, but something set in her mind, that she needed to continue to go forward on her own.

"Tamya, there is a God who sees and knows all that's going on in your life, even though it seems to be cloudy and unfixable. Your situation is going to change today! Everything that you have experienced is going to make you who you are about to become. You are all out of options. I can see the pain in your eyes—so deep and distant. You cry for help now. Whether you know it or not, you are finally tired and you are ready to trade in your old lifestyle for one worth living. I want you to do one thing."

"What's that?" Tamya asked.

"I want you to go home, gather your three children, get your Bible, and read aloud three times Psalms 91:1. Kiss and hug all three. Every time you feel mad or there is any other habit trying to come across your mind, read that chapter three times."

"What is that supposed to do? How can that help me?"

"It will start to feed the hungry spirit that wants to breathe in you. If you don't, you will die! As you continue to feed your soul, you must begin to pray. As you pray, even if you don't want to, the Lord will begin to deal with your heart. Remember, your soul is crying. It wants to live, that is your choice to feed it with life. Don't worry about what your children are having because it's already done."

"Why would you tell someone they will die if they don't do what you say?"

"Tamya, please just do it. You will get a better understanding later."

"Okay, but I still feel lost."

"I can promise you that once you read the verse three times, what you are feeling right now will fade," said Val.

"Thanks for your time!" Tamya replied. She got up and walked out of the office. As soon as she left, Val fell on the floor once more, crying and shaking as though it was twenty degrees in her office. She then fell asleep for twenty minutes. A knock on the door startled her awake. She did not remember falling asleep. It was Charity.

"Val, are you okay?" Charity asked.

"Yes, I think I fell asleep for a minute. I must have been really tired after that visit. It's like I used too much energy. I'm okay now, though. Give me minute while I get myself together," Val responded.

"When you are ready, Jermaine is here. Buzz me when you are ready."

"Okay, thanks." Val felt as if a part of her had walked out the door with the last client. It was a feeling she had never felt before. "Charity, I am ready for Jermaine," Val called out.

Jermaine walked inside Val's office and said, "Hey, Val. You look tired."

"I'm okay now. How are things going with you this week?" Val asked.

"Well, Val, it seems to be worse now more than ever."

"What do you mean?"

"Well, I asked her to go to church with me, but she just ignored me. Why is it that I am hurting so badly? I just want to leave her and give up on trying getting her to see the light. It's like I know we both started out in the street, but I have come around. Why is she holding a grudge so tough?"

"I want you to understand, Jermaine, that women are emotional sponges. We soak up everything. The things that you went through before you turned your life around has soaked up to the point that it has blinded her to the fact that the Lord has made you a new mind. She still sees you as the enemy and the man who once hurt her. Your pain is so hard because unlike a man, women cry more and release the painful emotions. That's why the pain for women is less overpowering once she gets over a man, because during the hurting times, she expresses the pain. Most men find activities and other things to release stress and pain. Some workout, some work long hours, some play sports. There seems to be more activities for a man to occupy his mind during his time of pain. It's different for a man who wants to make a relationship work in spite of his situation. He will have to endure each and every emotion since he has to stare his pain in the face every day to try to get it to cooperate. The one thing that is very important to you now is prayer. Instead of stressing and trying to change her, you have to stay focused and keep going in the right direction. The Lord will heal your family and fix your wife because the head of that body is now complete. As long as your heart is clean and your mind is clear, God can start to fix the broken vessels. Jermaine, you are a good man. You must know that if she is who the Lord has for you, then all will be well, but if the Lord wants to move her and send you in the direction of a godly woman, you need to accept his offer. You are going in the right direction. You will see God find favor in your commitment to him, and for that, he will

Serenity They Seek

reward you. I am so proud of you. You have truly changed. I gave you an advice one time and you ran with it. I know this is something you did not want to hear, but when you leave here today, I want you to trust God with everything that you have, from this day forward, and watch things happen. I have a feeling that when you come back next month, you would have become what you are here for."

"Ha-ha-ha, I know that I will!"

Val looked up at him quickly to see the expression on his face after he made that comment. Val Silently: Did he not hear what he just said? "That's right."

"Well, Val, thank you for helping me understand women. I will stop at Charity's desk and make my last appointment," said Jermaine. Val looked at him again. He looked like he was just talking normal. Val knew then that Jermaine was a soul she had witnessed to, and he accepted. When he walked out, Val rushed to her desk to write in her book, and as she began to write, she wrote down his last comment and signed it: Serenity.

"Val, your last appointment and walk-in is here," Charity said.

"Send him in," Val responded.

"Hello, Val?" Charles said as he walked in.

"Hello, Charles! How are you doing?" Val greeted.

"I guess I'm okay. I appreciate you seeing me in such a short notice. I heard about you through a lady at the unemployment office. I forgot her name."

"Would her name be Elizabeth?"

"No, I'm not sure. I think it starts with a K, but I do know it's not Elizabeth."

"My attention is all yours."

"I just feel a little frustrated," Charles confided.

"Why is that?" Val asked, concerned.

"I just can't seem to find a job. It's like everywhere I apply, they just won't even consider me for an interview. I have done everything that is required for me to qualify. I have got my GED, I have got me some clothes to wear, and my old partner has been cutting my hair on credit. I have actually been doing everything right, I think."

"So, why do you feel nothing is going to happen or already haven't?"

"Well, for one. I think it's because I am honest on my application."

"What do you mean honest?"

"Where the application asks if I ever was convicted of a felony, I answer yes. I have a felony. I only served fourteen months in prison."

"No need to go into details," said Val. "I understand where you are coming from."

"I just feel like giving up and getting back in the streets. I have two sons who I can't even provide for. I used to be able to buy them any and everything they needed and wanted, but now, I can't even buy them toilet paper for their house. I feel like a looser, like I have failed them and myself."

"It's not at all bad as you think. The hardest part has already come."

"What do you mean?"

"You have chosen to take all the steps to go in the right direction," Val started explaining. "Everything you have done is not only great but also preparing you for change. The feeling you have is normal during change. The only two things you lack are patience and hope, which leads you to faith."

"Faith comes from hope, what does that accomplish when no one will even review over my entire application? You only hope when they consider you for a position, or when you make it to the interview."

"See, that's where you are so shallow," answered Val. "Faith and hope are for things unseen or seems to be merely impossible to believe in. It only comes from God."

"But I don't even go to church. I have not been to church in over six years. How do you know the Lord even wants to help me?"

"Let me ask you a few questions. You really don't have to answer to me. Just let me ask them and then you answer them to yourself."

"What's that?" asked Charles.

"Are you still breathing? Do you have your health and strength? Are you out of prison? Do you think your children still love you even though you cannot physically buy them everything anymore?" Val asked. "If all of your answers are yes, then you still have a chance to change your life. Live for God and have faith for things you think are impossible. I know that you feel your luck is bad, but if you listen to your heart, you will hear the strength that is in active mode. If you continue to do the right things, something good is definitely going to come out of it. Giving up should no longer be an option."

"Why is it, when everyone starts having problems, they talk about God?"

"Because everyone who talks about him obviously knows where their help come from. Ha-ha! Not everybody believes. That is because when something is going wrong, they feel that God does not love them given that they are going through hard times. Sometimes, we can make decisions that will cause us to go through extremely tough times," replied Val. "God loves all of us, and he is the one we should always call on in our time of need. That should not be the only time we should call on him. We should call on him even when things are going great since you never know when danger is lurking right around the corner. You never know if your past decisions are going to come back to haunt you. You are never in the clear of dangerous situations, but you can go around each and every one of them in your path by God's grace. You must put him first in everything you do. That way, danger cannot come in and tear you down for a moment. Charles, you are going in the correct path, and everyone whom you come across with knows it. Some will accept you and some will reject you, but you must always remember that the only one who can make a change is God himself."

"I can't tell if everyone sees it."

"I can," said Val without hesitation. "That's why whoever sent you here cared enough to send you to me for the confirmation of your effort."

"Hey, you are right. I have been going to that office every day for two months straight, but I had never seen that woman," Charles said. "I know now she had been sitting in the desk behind the lady I was seeing. Somehow, she had been seeing me. She stopped me the other day and told me that someone is going to give me a job soon. Until then, she gave me your card and said, 'Go and see this lady. She will help you keep your mind open until you find your way.'"

"Don't think she is the only one who wants to see you prosper. You are loved by many, though you don't even know they care."

"Thank you, Mrs. Valoria. You have really been a big help to me."

"That's Miss, and you are more than welcome," corrected Val. "I am in the business for helping people."

"Would it be okay if I come back if I feel frustrated later about anything?"

"Sure, since you came in today, you would not be considered a walk-in anymore. It will be best if you make an appointment. That way, I can make sure, I am here during your time of need."

"Okay, Val, thanks."

When Charles left, Valoria sat at her desk and prayed for about thirty minutes. As she began to raise her head up, her phone rang and startled her. "This is Valoria," Val answered. No one said anything, but before she hung up, she heard a very faint sigh. Val then went into her desk and pulled out her folder with all of her most important documents. While she scrambled through trying to find what she was looking for, she stopped and looked at the phone, trying to figure out why she had gotten a silent call again. Val had never had experienced prank calls on her business phone.

As she left her office for the day, she stopped at Charity's desk and gave her two envelopes already sealed and addressed. "Could you please drop these in the mailbox on your way home, Char? Also, call Elizabeth at the unemployment office and have her call me on my cell," Val told Charity.

"Val, could you please stop worrying about people and go home and relax with your son?" Charity said.

"I don't worry about people, Char, that's why I like the type of work I do, because worrying is one thing, I am free from." She smiled at Charity and left.

Val finally made it home, and as soon as she walked through the door, her sister was already there with Val's son, who was ten years old. His name was Isaac. He was one of the most well-mannered children you would ever meet, and he was very smart and very protective of his mom. Isaac ran straight to her with a picture he had drew for her.

"Hi, Momma. How was your day?" Isaac asked excitedly.

"Even better now that I am at home with you. You are my fuel," Val responded.

"I know, Momma. You fill up with love every time I give you a hug."

Val soon got settled, cooked dinner, and prepared her and Isaac for the next day. A lot of people did not know Val's personal life. She always kept that portion of her distanced from everything else. Val was a divorced, now a single, woman living without worry or want. On her bedroom door, she had a saying written in big gold letters: THE LORD IS MY SHEPHERD AND MY SALVATION. I SHALL NOT WANT.

Val woke up the next morning with an even bigger smile on her face. On her way to the office, her cell phone rang. It was Elizabeth. Val stayed on the phone with Elizabeth for about ten minutes before walking to the office. When she finally walked in and sat down, there was a knock on the door. "Come in," Val said. To her surprise, it was a face she did not think she would ever see again. It was Antwan, Allen's son. "Hello, Antwan, it's good to see you," she greeted.

"Yeah, same to you, too! Hey, look, even though it's late, I want to apologize for the way I acted last time I was here," Antwan said.

"Oh, don't worry about it. I forgave you before I lay down and went to sleep that night."

"I just came here because I wanted to ask you something."

"And what might that be?" asked Val.

"Do you think that a thug can really change and stay out of the streets?"

"Yes, I do. As a matter of fact, I can tell you one I know right now."

"Who?"

"Your father," answered Val.

"I thought you were going to really tell me one. My father has never been a real thug."

"And why is that, because he is not young anymore? Or is it because he didn't listen to the same music as you?"

"No, it's because he got out of it and stayed away too easy," replied Antwan. "He doesn't really have any war scars or a huge criminal record. I can go in the city and call every police officer by their first name. That's how rowdy I've been."

"I used to hear about your father all the time in the streets when I was younger," Val said. "I even remembered his street name. Let me tell you what I heard about him. They called him AL Smooth. I used to wonder why they called him that, so I asked someone who knew more about him. He told me it was because everything that was smooth, bad or good, was him. The reason he didn't see the jail a lot was because he had people going for him. Your dad had all of the women—even the younger girls wanted to ride in his cars. I remember hearing about all of the fights in the clubs over him. He once got so bad that he had a whole city on lock with every type of drugs you could buy. He was so smart. He had a gun license, so everyone knew he was the only thug on the block who had a permit to be strapped. If the police pulled him over or even attempted to suspect him, he had an alibi all the time. He helped a few people get their businesses started when he was coming up, so they had his back and even had him clocked in at their business while he was still in the bed. Now, if that's not a thug you have never seen before, that's one."

"If he had it that well, why did he get out?" asked Antwan, surprised.

"Maybe because he took heed to his first warning," Val responded, "and the Lord made a way of escape for him. It almost came to an end for your father and his reputation. All of his money eventually faded while looking for a job and trying to continue the best life for you, I do remember.

"Antwan, the Lord will give you a warning before self-destruction. That warning can be in so many ways. By a close call or someone talking to you or even the conscience to go a different direction; I even truly believe that we get more than one warning. Have you ever felt funny about something and it seems like everything that day seems weird? If your mind is open and you listen to your heart real close, it will almost be screaming a warning to you."

"I understand where you are coming from, but that does not mean that what you are saying can happen to anybody. I believe that whatever is meant to happen, will happen."

"That is true, but the bad choices we make, we often have a conscience before we do it," continued Val. "That right there is a sign that even though it's going in my path bad, the Lord does not want anything bad to happen to us, so that conscience acts as a shield to protect us from making the wrong decision. We, as human beings, try ourselves or sometimes, we don't believe there is something far greater than us, so we go off on our own human nature and judgment. You can be walking down a long colorful hallway, and as you get to the corner, a sign reads STOP HERE NOW. When you turn the corner and walk to the next corner, the walls will turn grey, and the floor will fall in. Now, because of our curiosity as humans, some of us will turn the corner in disbelief of what it is saying just to see the physical sight of what the sign has warned us about. We turn and see that the hall is even longer than the first one, so we feel it will be impossible to see that other corner. Now, one thing that we forgot to include in that curiosity was that the sign did not say how long it would be until we got to the next corner. It just said 'when you get there.' Some of us would stop there out of common sense, not by faith at this point. The other majority of us will continue walking just until we see the corner, then we will stop. So those who keep walking get to the corner where it is in sight. We see the darkness that lies right behind it, and just as soon as we turn around, it's too late. The floor underneath is gone, and there is no turning back. That symbolizes one hole we have fallen in, when all we had to do was stop at the warning post. So, you don't have to always come to the fall before you wake up. Sometimes, avoid that wrong path as many times as you can. God loves you, Antwan, and there is no reason why it could not be just as easy for you to walk away. You must also think about the fact that the sign also did not read how close you had to be to the other corner for you to feel its effects. You can be far from it and still fall in before time."

"I feel you well, Ms. Val. Thank you for talking to me in such short notice. I wish I could stay and talk to you a little longer, but I really have to go. Maybe I'll call and make an appointment to come back."

"Anytime, and remember that hall, don't go any further when it says stop."

"I won't! Bye!" Antwan left.

Valoria then went to her desk and signed onto her laptop. As she began to type, the phone rang. "Hello, this is Valoria," She answered.

"Hello, Val, this is your old schoolmate, Shy," the caller said.

"Cheryl?"

"Yep, it's me."

"Hey, girl, what's going on? I haven't heard from you since I moved out of the area. How have you been? How is the family?"

"Everyone is okay I guess."

"You guess?" Val asked.

"I was wondering if you have a few minutes to talk to me," Cheryl said.

"Now, girl, you know I will make time to talk to you." Cheryl was a white woman who was married to a black man. She had three beautiful boys with her husband. When Valoria met Cheryl, she was very quiet and did not talk a lot. So, Valoria started calling her Shy, and that has been her nickname every since. "So, what would you like to talk about?"

"Well, I wanted to know what you have planned for your birthday," Cheryl replied.

"Oh really, and why is my birthday so important to you this year?"

"I just thought it would be nice for me to plan something for you."

"Aww! That would be nice and all, but wouldn't you want to do something like that as a surprise?"

"You are right. I guess I am stalling away from what I really called to talk about."

Then, Val heard a small sniffle. "Cheryl, are you alright?" Val asked.

"I don't know, Val. I kind of want to let my marriage go."

"What's wrong, sweetie? You know I am here for you. You can talk to me about anything."

Right after Valoria said that, Charity stuck her head through the door and said softly, "I need to see you a minute," so Valoria told Cheryl to hold on.

"What's up, Charity?" Val asked.

"I just wanted you to know that a really fine gentleman came by here just a second ago, looking for you. He would not leave his name. He just told me that he would come back, and that it was important for him to see you. I thought that you should know, just in case you might know who he is. You could perhaps get in contact with him since he said it's important," Charity replied.

"I'm sorry, Charity, but I know just about enough as you know."

"Oh, well, I'm sorry for interrupting," replied Charity. "I just thought you should know before I go to lunch. He did not want to leave his name."

"Thanks, Charity, have a good one," Val said to Charity, then she went back to the phone. "Hello, I'm back. Why would you want to give up something that you have worked so hard to keep?"

"You would think that after all these years and three kids, his family would have accepted me by now," answered Shy. "His mother hates me for no reason, and his sister talks about me in front of my kids. I overheard my boys talking to each other about what they should do about their auntie talking about their mom."

"Did they hear everything she said about you, word for word?"

"To be honest, I don't know what they heard or hear. They won't tell me, trying to protect my feelings. I have never given them a reason to hate me, but I feel that because I am white, they have a problem with me and always will. I feel that I can have an army of children by him and they would still never accept me for me."

"What does Chris say and think about it?"

"He thinks I am overreacting, as usual," replied Shy. "He says that they don't have a problem with me, and I have believed that for the fourteen years I have been married to him, but for some reason, the feeling of me not being wanted is never left, and I never talked to anyone about it. Even though his oldest son has grown now, his son's mother is still at every family function. It's like they wish he had married her instead. She is black, of course. Every time I have said something to him about being uncomfortable, he assures me that I am his wife, whether they like it or not. He says he does not care what they say or think about our family, as long as I know he loves me. I must say he is supportive and loves me, but I still feel like there is something missing. And out of all the years, this is the year I feel it strongly more than ever."

"It sounds to me that you have pain that has been following you for years, and in order for you to heal from this pain, you are going to have to throw away the past," Val said to her friend. She continued. "As you said, for some reason, it is stronger now than ever before, maybe because you have reached a point in your life where you cannot take anymore. I know that what I'm about to say will sound like the hardest thing for you to do, but you are going to have to start by forgiving them. If, in fact, they do and always have had a problem with you, that is something they probably will never admit, so even though you don't know, you must forgive them anyway. That, to me, is the start of a healing process from all of the hurt you feel. That is the desperate feeling of being rejected and not accepted. No one likes to feel left out or last all the time. The one thing that I did hear you say, and that is actually good, is that you have not given them a reason not to like you. That should clarify to you that you are not the one with the problem. Any problem that they have with you is just that: their problem. I know you are a family person, and you would like nothing more than to feel loved by your family and his, but there is one thing I want you to always remember. Not everyone will love you, and not everyone will like you. There will always be people out there who will be the total opposite of what you want and need. When everyone else seems to be against you, always remember that God is always there for you, for the Lord made all mankind, black and white, and so on. So, where we, humans, put one another in a class, to God, we are all the same. I want you to always remember that, no matter what. Even if people point out that you are a white woman married to a black man, you can say in response to that 'I am a woman married to a man.' That's how God sees me, and that's that. Besides, if his family wants to be shallow and not love the person you are, they are missing out on more than a blessing. They are missing out on one of the best friends and family member one can ask for. You are special, and it shows to those who are not blinded by a lie."

"It always amazes me, Val, that you always know what to say to make a person feel better," Cheryl said.

"It's not me. It's what I represent, and God, who I believe in, keeps me going every day."

"I need to come and start going to the church you go to, so that I can become strong like you."

"It does not come overnight, and it is not the church you go to. It is how much church you allow to come into you and how much you practice what is in your heart," replied Val. "What most people fail to realize is that every time you make a bad choice, you must know that whatever that choice is, it is in your heart. You will hear people say, 'God looks at your heart,' but do they say your actions are led by your heart? The more you think of it that way, the less bad choices you will make because when it is there and you don't act on it is a way of telling the Lord you don't want it there."

"You are right. I will always remember that and use that every day. Thanks, Val. Oh yeah, you still did not tell me what you are doing on your birthday."

"Who knows, I might be married and gone on a cruise by then. Ha-ha-ha."

"Well, call me when you decide what you are going to do! I love you, Val, and I will talk to you later."

When Val hung up the phone, Charity had just made it back from lunch. It was almost time for Val to leave. Charity came in with a bag for Val.

"What's that you have there?" Val asked.

"Just something special for you, that's all," Charity replied.

"I'm so amazed. What is it?"

"You know that 50-dollar candle you saw the other day and said you did not have time to stop and buy it?"

"You didn't!"

"I did—because you deserve it—and when was the last time someone gave you a gift?"

"This morning."

"From who? And what was it?" Charity asked.

"Jesus," Val replied, "and it's the breath that I am breathing now."

The day was now over for Val. She decided to go to the gym and work off some tension for a few hours. When she turned in the plaza where the gym was, she noticed an old lady crossing the street. She did not have time to look closely, so she parked first. When Val got out of the car, she swallowed very hard because standing behind her car was the little old woman from the grocery store. She had on old clothes again; this time, with a different, up-to-date tote bag. She stood there and stared at Val for a minute then smiled and walked off. Val raised her eyebrows this time because that was the only action the lady had made since the last time she had seen her. As the lady walked off, Val yelled out, "Hello, how are you today?"

The old lady responded without turning around, "Never better."

Val thought then, more than ever, that the lady was a little strange, but she, in no way, treated her like a stranger. She spoke even though she felt a little uneasy. When Val went into the gym, she noticed that the instructor was extremely happy to see her. Her name was Jenna.

"Hello, Jenna. What's going great with you?" Val greeted.

"Everything, now that you have walked through the door," Jenna replied.

"Well, okay, thanks for that welcome."

"The reason I say that is because there is a lady here, I want you to meet."

"Okay," Val responded. Jenna then grabbed Val's hand and led her over to a woman who was about 5'8" in height; she was light skinned with bumps all over her face. Her hair was broken off really bad, and she was a little overweight. She looked as if she was in a size-ten shoe, and she had really saggy breasts. She had really thin facial features. She looked very different.

"Hey, Leia, I want you to meet Valoria," Jenna told the lady.

"Hello, Valoria," the lady greeted Val.

"Hi," Val replied.

"Ms. Leia here asked me if I knew a counselor, and I told her I did, but I didn't have your number so I couldn't call you. I did think I would see you a whole lot sooner than today," Jenna told Val.

"How long has it been?" Val asked.

"About two months. I remembered as soon as you walked through the door. What's really puzzling me is that I haven't seen you since then, either, Leia, since that day," Jenna said.

"Well, you know what they say, things happen for a reason. People are put in your path just for purposes," Val explained.

"Well, now that you two have met, I need to go help someone burn off those pounds," Jenna said.

When Jenna walked off, Val looked back at Leia, and she noticed Leia had her head down. Val could tell that self-love did not live there. "Did you drop something?" Val asked.

Leia looked up quickly. "No, it's just a habit," Leia responded.

"Well, I'm going to tell you now: that is the worst habit of all, looking down. I'm not trying to sound harsh. I just want you to keep that in mind. Why don't you come and join me on the treadmill?"

"Well, I don't know. It seems that you are too good for me to hang out with."

Val turned around in disbelief when she had said that. "If you honestly feel that I am a better person than you, then you stay right here," Val said. As she turned to walk away, she noticed that Leia did not move. Val thought if she put a little fire under her that would make her at least cooperate. She then noticed it was far worse than she knew. She got to the treadmill, turned around, and noticed that Leia was headed toward the door. Val then turned and ran out after her. "Wait!" she called out.

"Wait for what?" replied Leia.

"I did not mean it the way that you took it. I was hoping that you know within yourself that I am not better than you."

"But you are, you are very pretty and your body is in shape. You have no bumps on your face and you have a beautiful smile. Don't act like you don't see that I am not cute. Please don't ask me how I know, uhhh, it's probably because everyone has always talked about me. Even my own family has named me the ugly duckling of my sisters. I'm just so tired of being made fun of, or looked at funny when I am out by myself. I don't care what you say. I wanted to talk to someone two months ago. It does not matter to me how I feel anymore. I wish she had never brought you over to me."

"Well, I'm glad she did," said Val. "What I see is a beautiful woman."

"Oh, please, don't come to me with that beauty-is-in-the-eye-of-the-beholder crap because I'm not listening," Leia said vehemently. "That is a counselor's line."

"Behold the beauty that is not in the eye," Val said. Leia turned and looked at Val, as if she had just given her a diamond. "If I did not care or thought I was better than you, I would not be standing out here talking to you. I would have stayed in the gym and enjoyed my workout. But you, as a person in need, are more important to me right now. I see the pain in your eyes, and I feel they want to be something you imagine is better. Leia, you are what you are named. You may not see what I see, but under all of that pain and shame, I see a magnificent woman." Leia was a woman who had hated who she was for years, a woman who should appreciate who God made her. "Did you know that whatever you feel on the inside can affect your appearance on the outside?"

"Right."

"Well, in case you did not know, you know now."

"So, I guess if I feel fat, then that's what made me fat."

"No, when you are unhappy on the inside, it will reflect on the outside. Everybody's stress is different. Some people deal with stress negatively, and some deal with it in a positive way." Leia started to cry. "It's okay to cry. That is how pressure is released. If you hold on to the pressure, it will build up and turn into a path of depression. You are so much more than that. You are just beautiful, and maybe even more beautiful than me, if you would let your shield down," Val comforted.

"How can you say that when you don't even know me like that?"

"I may not know you physically, but I do recognize that attitude. I do feel the negative power coming from you." As the sun began to set, it started to sprinkle a little bit. "Do you have more time to talk?" Val asked.

"Not really. I have to get ready to go to work. I work third shift at the hospital," Leia answered.

"Oh really, what do you do?"

"I am a nurse practitioner."

"Wow, great career," said Val.

"Yeah, well, when you don't have a life and no one wants to be bothered with you, what else can you do but go to school?" replied Leia flippantly. "I like helping people, but that is not the field that I dream of retiring from."

"No? Well, what is it that you really want to do?" Valoria asked.

"Real estate, but I am not pretty enough."

"I really would like for you to come and see me tomorrow. Is it possible?"

"I don't know. I can try."

"Look, here is the address and the hours I will be in. In fact, here is my cell number. You can either show up or call me and let me know when you can. I am a single parent, so after 6:30 P.M., I have to play that part in my life."

"Thanks, I'll try."

"Please," said Val. "Not for me, but for the real Leia. It's time for you to shine like the jewel you are."

A tear fell from Leia's face as she opened her car door. She got in then drove off. At that time, around 5:00 P.M., Val just got back in her car and went home. She just decided to get on her treadmill at home. The only reason she went to the gym was to have a different surrounding and no distractions from her son. On her way home, she could do nothing but think about the young lady, Leia, and wonder what she did on a daily basis.

The next morning, Val woke up, and her son was in her bed. "Isaac?"

"I had a bad dream, Momma, so I came in here so I could sleep," Isaac said. She gave him a kiss on his forehead and got up to get them both ready for the day.

On her way to the office, Val decided to stop at Walgreens and get herself some honey-roasted peanuts. When she was coming out of the store, her cell phone rang. It was Charity calling.

"Hey, boss, where are you? Jermaine is here. He said it's important that he speaks with you before he goes to work," Charity said.

"Okay, let him know I'm just down the street. I will be there in five minutes," Val replied.

Val finally arrived at the office. As soon as she got off the elevator and entered into the office, she saw Jermaine sitting in the waiting area. She noticed a change in his attitude. He was smiling. "Come on in my office, Jermaine. I know you have to be at work soon," Val said.

"I did what you advised, and things are definitely better," Jermaine replied.

"Well, good."

"She finally sat down and talked to me," said Jermaine excitedly. "She told me that she can't believe I have changed, and that she is scared that I might hurt her again. She did agree to start going to church with me, but the most wonderful thing of all is that when I went to sleep last night, I heard her get on her knees and pray for the Lord to give her a sign, that I am really a changed man. I don't think I was supposed to hear her prayer, but since I did, I know that she really loves me. She is just scared that I might turn back into the person I was before. I came to you to get some advice on what I should do to show her I love her more than ever and that I want it to last forever."

"That is an answer I cannot give you. The hardest part now is convincing her you have changed like you say you have. That can only come from your heart. I really believe you should pray more now."

"Why?"

"Because its sounds to me you have a hard time accepting your change," answered Val. "I don't mean that in a bad way, but you should just trust your own judgment, and know that the Lord is walking with you, every step of the way. If you have never been that man to show affection, I am going to tell you to follow every good feeling that comes into your mind, as long as it will please God. It will eventually come naturally because it will be in you more than ever."

"What if she starts to change?" Jermaine asked.

"She won't change. As long as you stay focused and on the right path, she will soon line directly up with you, and besides, if you really want your marriage to work and it's in God's will, then nothing can change destiny," Val said.

"Oh my, look at the time. I really must get going."

"Jermaine, it's going to get better. God has already answered your prayers."

"I know he has!" Jermaine exclaimed. While walking out the door, Val smiled because, as she had already noted, that was one life she had made an impact on. Jermaine was referred to her from a church member of the church she attended. He was going to seek marriage counseling, but his wife would not agree to come, so he came alone. Because of his determination to save his marriage, he carried the weight on his own and eventually was able to reach her through his own faith, and that God was going to heal his marriage.

A month had passed, but Val had not heard from Jermaine. When she got to the office, she asked Charity if she had any messages. Charity told her she had none, but she did hear her line ring earlier, which was strange because it normally came through Charity first. She went in her office and noticed she missed two phone calls: the first one from Jermaine and the second one from Leia, who she had not heard from since she talked to her last at the gym. As bad as she wanted to call Leia first, she decided it would be fair to call them in the order that they called. "Good morning, Jermaine. How are you?" Val called Jermaine.

"Hello, Val, I know you have not heard from me in a while, and that's because things are going great," Jermaine said. Val smiled. "My wife has joined the church and we just found out yesterday that we are expecting another baby. I just had to call and tell you the good news and to say thank you for everything you have done. I thank God because he allowed you to help me. Thanks, Val, and the next time I talk to you, it will be just to update you on my happiness." Val was so excited to hear that everything was going the way Jermaine had prayed for it to go. She was so eager to call Leia, but right as she put her hand on the phone receiver, the phone rang. "This is Valoria," Val said.

"This is Allen. He's gone, Val. I need to come see you tomorrow. I just can't seem to want to talk to anyone else."

"Who's gone, Allen?" Val asked, confused.

"Antwan," replied Allen. "He was shot and killed two days ago. When I last talked to him, he told me he had come and talked to you on his own. He told me he was going to come back this week because you told him some things that made him think about changing his lifestyle. He just didn't make it. It's too late, Val." Allen began to cry on the phone.

"Allen, I am so sorry." A tear fell down Val's face. She then began to remember what she last told Antwan, and she thought out loud by mistake and said, 'He walked to the second corner.'"

Allen then said, "What? How do you know? Tell me how you know, Val."

"I'm sorry. I was thinking out loud. I don't know anything."

"Oh, I thought you heard. He had just left my house to go to the store. He said he had to stop at his mother's house. His friend, Andre, told me that he stopped at his house, too. He said his phone rang, and instead of him going straight down the street to his mother's house, he went around the corner, and that's the last anyone seen him alive. They shot my son in the head, twice, and in the chest, six times. When they found him, he had his phone on speed dial to my cell number. He was going to try to call me and say goodbye. I know he was, Val."

"You will be fine. Just come and see me tomorrow."

"I will be there about 10 A.M."

"That's fine," Val said. She then opened the door to her office to tell Charity to put Allen on the schedule. When she looked out the door, inexpertly, Charity stood straight up as though she was doing something, she had no business doing.

"Hey, Val!" Charity said, surprised.

"What are you doing? Why are you so jumpy?" Val pried.

"You just startled me. That's all."

"Oh, okay, well, I'm sorry for popping in on you. I just want you to put Allen on my schedule for tomorrow."

"Oh, okay. Val?" Charity asked hesitantly.

"Yes?"

"Are you busy right now?"

"No, not really, what's up?"

"You have a walk-in," Charity said. Charity then pointed over by the elevators where the magazines were.

"Why didn't you buzz me and let me know?"

"Well, I saw your light on, so I assumed that you were on the phone."

"Oh, okay, where is he?" Val asked. As she peaked around the corner, she had seen that it was Zack.

Zack greeted, "Hey, Val, there you are. I finally get to see you."

Val instantly got sick to her stomach. "Come on in," she said.

As Val was walking back to her office, Charity mumbled under her voice, "He is fine." Val just looked at her and gave her a fake smile.

"Well, hello, Zack, how are you?" Val asked.

"I'm fine, except I have this problem."

"And what could that be?"

"I am addicted to pretty women," answered Zack with a straight face.

"Zack, this is my business, not a dating game."

"I know. That's why I need your help because I'm a sex addict, and I can't control the way I feel about pretty women. There is this one whom I can't take my mind off. I even had dreams of being her man."

"It's called lust, Zack. You have a large lustful appetite for women. A lot of men have that problem. The only person who can help you with that is Jesus."

"I know," said Zack. "That's why he sent me to you. He told me you could help me get over these feelings."

"I honestly don't know what to tell you on that. You have to pray that the Lord removes that lust from you and helps you control your responses to the way you feel."

"So, why are you in the position you are in, if you can't help me?" Then, Zack got up, locked Val's door, and sat back down. "You see, Val, even as I am sitting here talking to you, I can't control the way I am feeling." He then began to take off his shirt and rub his stomach. He was very well built up. He was a very attractive man, no doubt.

"I would appreciate if you do not get undressed in my office. You are wrong for what you are doing," Val said.

"So, what will make it right, Val?"

"If you take one minute to put your shirt on and get out of my office—"

"You are not a godly woman. If you can't help me, you can't help anyone." While he was putting on his shirt, he turned to Val and said, "I'll see you later, Val."

"No, you won't, not until you pray for self-control first," replied Val as calmly as she could.

When Zack left, Val ran out of the office to the bathroom. When she got to the bathroom, she began to throw up. As she was throwing up, she started to pray that whatever illness was trying to come down on her would go away.

When she returned to her office, Charity came in with a cup of water. "Are you okay, Val? I heard you at my desk from the bathroom. Are you pregnant?"

Val looked at Charity as if she wanted to throw up again, but what she had said was, "No, I'm not pregnant. I just got sick all of a sudden."

"Maybe someone came in here with a virus and did not tell you they were sick."

"I don't know, but this sickness just feels a little weird. I don't know, maybe it was something I ate. I feel better now, though. I think it will be best if I did not drink anything at this point."

"Okay, but if it is okay, I will feel better if I could leave your door open for the rest of the day, so that I can keep an eye on you."

"That's fine, but if I get a walk-in, I will have to close the door, or if I get an important phone call, I will need no distractions."

"Agreed."

Val sat at her desk for a minute, thinking about where this sickness came from, and then, she remembered she needed to call Leia back, which she did.

"Hello," Leia said, answering Val's call.

"Hello, Leia, this is Val returning your call," Val said.

"Yes, thank you for calling me back. I have been thinking about some things that you said to me, and I was wondering if the invitation to come and talk to you is still open."

"Most definitely," Val assured her. "Anytime I extend an offer, as long as I have breath in my body, there is no expiration. How have you been?"

"I guess I could be a whole lot better, if I had talk to you sooner."

"Don't dwell on what you feel you should have done because some things don't and can't happen overnight. Look at it as if it was not time for you to talk to me. Maybe it was just meant for you to know I'm here."

"I guess you can call it that way," said Leia. "I think I am back in my way of wanting to do something about my situation. I'm just tired of being the way that I am. Believe it or not, I used to be skinny when I was little."

"Why do you feel like you have to justify your situation?"

"I just do."

"Leia, you don't," insisted Val. "I want you to come and see me tomorrow. If possible, I really don't want to take no for an answer."

"I guess I can make it by."

"Great, would around lunch be okay?"

"Sure, I'm on your busy schedule."

"I only have one client I know of tomorrow, so I will have plenty of time to talk to you, if you are still interested."

"Okay, I will be there tomorrow around lunch." Then, they hung up.

Calvin Rucker lived in Boston, Massachusetts. Calvin was a man of God. He was a man who prayed every day. Calvin strived and lived his life in holiness. The one thing that really stood out about Calvin was that he waited and trusted in the Lord. Calvin was an extremely handsome man. He was about 6'2" and had a light-brown complexion. His body weight and his hands and feet were perfectly matched to frame. It seemed as though he was molded well together. He had a smile that really stood out. His eyes and nose were perfectly centered on his face. His voice was deep, but humble. He had the kind of a sophisticated street savvy about him. Calvin had a very interesting career; he was a computer analyst for the government. Calvin had been with the government since he had been out of college. When he was in college, he did play football. He was one of the most popular guys in school, all four years. He dated the prettiest women. Calvin had one son from a previous relationship, before he turned his life over to the Lord.

Calvin was leaving Bible study one Wednesday Night. He and another brother named Charles stopped and talked in the parking lot, before Charles's wife came out. "What's going on, man?" Calvin greeted Charles.

"Awww, man, just waiting for the play-offs to roll around, so I can kill some time until Londa has the baby," Charles responded.

"I can't ask you if are you ready to be a father because it is too late," said Calvin. "So, what I should be asking you is: how's your preparation coming?"

"Man, God is amazing," Charles replied. "I'm still amazed how the Lord can take a seed, plant it in a woman, and it grows into a human being. The soul was planted when the seed was sown. I just thank God that I'm not still in those streets. God knows what my wife would be dealing with if I were still in the streets. Man, last Friday night, she woke up at 1:00 A.M., coughing and holding her stomach like she was about to choke to death. This time last year, you know I was in the street at 1:30 A.M., just now getting hyped. You know, Cal, I thank God that he allowed you to be my friend at that time. Because of you, I was able to find my own way to God. If you had not invited me to the brotherhood service, I would not have ever known that there was something way greater than drugs, women, cars, and jewelry. You know, man, you have been in church for four years now, and you still are by yourself. I don't know if you even want a wife yet, but I have been praying that the Lord sends you in the direction of what you need in your life."

"Ha-ha, thanks, man, but the first two years, I dedicated all of my time getting my relationship with God together, but for these last two years, I think I am ready for a wife," said Calvin amicably. "I know that I have grown spiritually, and that the Lord will guide me to her, but for now, I have to be patient. I have a few friends now whom I have met at the conventions, but right now, God have not told me if any of them is the one. So, patiently, I must wait. It's been really hard for me, but I know once I say I do, all of my frustrations will go away."

"Ha-ha-ha-ha, that is the truth," agreed Charles.

"Hey, guys, what's going on over here?" Yolanda, Charles's wife, interrupted.

"Hey, sis. Just standing around minding our business, that's all," Calvin said.

"Excuse me!" Yolanda said, irritated.

"Just kidding, hey, y'all, have a good evening!" Calvin said.

"Ha-ha-ha-ha, all right man, we will see you on Sunday," Charles answered.

"Always!" Calvin went home and prepared himself a snack before he got ready to go to bed. After ironing his clothes for tomorrow, doing 200 pushups, showering, and laying down for bed, Calvin got on his knees and began to pray. "Lord, tonight, I come to you not only as a child of God, but as a man in the flesh, asking for a companion. You said in your word that a man that findeth a wife findeth a good thing. I need your help and your direction in my search. I think maybe I have been praying the wrong prayer from time to time. I have been asking you to send me a wife. I know now that, as a man, I can't wait for you to send her to me. I have to go out and find her. Lord, as I begin my search, be with me. Thank you for keeping me this far. I love you, Lord. Amen."

That night, while Calvin was asleep, an angel came to him and whispered in his ear. To Calvin, it was as if his dream was blank. He could only hear a sound. As he frowned in his sleep, he heard a woman's voice. The voice sounded very soft, sweet, and full of love. It was the voice of a woman he had never heard before. The voice said softly, "You know Momma loves her baby." After he heard the voice, he woke up and sat straight up in bed. He then got up to get some Gatorade. While he was standing in his kitchen, he was trying to figure out where he had heard that voice before. *He thought, I never heard my child's mother say that in my presence. I don't remember my mother saying it that way to me. I just wish I knew what that dream was.* Calvin then went back to bed and thought nothing else on that voice.

Val finished up her day by filing notes in her important file. Val went home and prepared a healthy meal for her and her son. When they finished eating, she began cleaning up her house. While she was busy cleaning, her phone rang. "Hello?" she answered.

"Hey, girl, what would you know?" It was Jonathan, Valoria's ex-husband and the father of her child. "Where is my seed?"

"He is taking a shower, getting ready for tomorrow. You know what time he goes to bed. Why are you calling so late?"

"It should not be a time limit on me calling my son, but I will respect his sleep. Since he is not asleep, I should be able to call."

"Well, he does not allow me in the bathroom when he is in there, so you are going to have to try back later." Val had had a previous, trying past with this man. He was not the best man for her, so she decided a long time ago to let him go. Val actually left him before she got her life right with God. Right after she left him, she struggled with loneliness and a few men whom she leaned on as a shoulder to cry on. Val had since then understood that she was never going to be happy until she straightened out her life. She knew that she was going to have to let everyone whom she dealt with go, so she could start to focus on what she needed to do in her life. He was one of the deadweights she had to let go. Val had truly loved this man once before. She actually loved him more than she loved herself at one time.

"What time does he get out of school?" Jonathan asked.

"Why? Are you going to surprise me and pick him up?"

"No, I have something to do, but I do want to come by and see him when y'all get back home."

"I don't think that is going to be possible tomorrow," replied Val, "because he is going with my sister to the bowling alley tomorrow night with her friend's nephew."

"Whatever, Val, that's cool. I'll just come by later that night, when he gets back home."

"Why don't you just wait until this weekend when he has nothing to do, and that will give me a few hours of free time to myself? And besides, wouldn't your girlfriend want to know where you are at 10:00 P.M.?"

"So, you telling me he won't be back until then?" asked Jonathan.

"Yeah!"

"Well, I will come then. I am a grown man. I do what I want to do. Like I have told you before, she is not my girlfriend. She's just cool."

"Wow! Okay, Johnny, why don't you call me tomorrow and we will see."

"Whatever, Val."

Val pulled in the garage and noticed a blue Lexus with rims on it. *Hmm, she thought to herself, who could this be? I don't have any clients who are big like this. They are parked in my visitor's space. Maybe Charity got herself a boyfriend.* When Val got off the elevator, she began to walk toward Charity's desk, and she noticed a man signing in as a walk-in. As she approached, he turned around to greet the footsteps. It was Zack, standing there looking like a million bucks. "Hello, Val, I think I am really ready now," Zack said.

"Well, I am glad you really want to talk this time. Did you pray for what I asked you too last time?" Val asked.

"Sure, I did!" Zack responded.

"Good, come in my office." Zack then turned, looked at Charity, and smiled innocently. When they got in Val's office, Zack sat in the chair and positioned himself like he was untouchable. "Nice ride you have. You seem to be living a successful life."

"I try, but I still lack so much. I have extremely nice things. As a matter of fact, I feel like I have worked so hard all my life. I deserve the best."

"And you should feel like that for yourself because when you do the right things and strive for the best, you will soon get what you want to achieve, and sometimes, more than you deserve. So, I agree with you. Hard work pays off."

"Thanks!"

"What can I help you with today, Zack?" Val asked.

"I know you probably think I am crazy, Val, but I seriously have a problem and an addiction to women," Zack replied.

"I don't think you are crazy," said Val. "It's just that when you were here last time, I did not think you were serious about wanting to address your problem. By you coming back, that lets me know you really want to get help. I understand you want to know why you feel this way all of the time."

"Exactly," Zack said. Val went behind her desk and pulled out her notepad. When she opened her desk drawer, she felt a little light-headed and queasy at her stomach. She frowned, unaware that she was frowning, but Zack had seen her facial expression. He asked, "Are you alright, Val?"

"Yes, I'm fine," she said. "I think I turned to fast or something. I'll be fine. Now, where were we?"

"You were saying I want to understand why I am like this."

"Oh yeah! For one, I would like to say that it is perfectly normal to have a high sex drive at your age. But what's making you think you have a problem?"

"Well, for one, I daydream more than normal. I have a habit that I practice every day, to try to make as much of my feelings go away."

"Stop right there," Val said urgently. "I know what you are talking about, so, you really don't have to go into details."

"Well, what I am trying to say is, the reason I don't have a girlfriend or a wife is because I have not found a woman who can deal with me and my huge appetite."

"Unfortunately, you are in that category of being extremely hot natured. Because of it, it has caused you to yearn for more than your body can handle. Once it reaches that point, it starts to affect everything you do. It will have you thinking about nature while you are eating your dinner or doing something totally opposite from what you are thinking about. Your whole life will then accommodate your habit."

"You are right," said Zack. "I'm always trying to be sexy in any way that I can. I know that I am a handsome man, with a lot going for myself, but I need a woman in my life." As he proceeded to talk, he then began to take off his jacket and lay back on the chair. When he swung his jacket across the arm of the chair, Val caught a whiff of his cologne. She instantly raised her eyebrows because that smell was like honey, and she was a bee. She stood and began to walk around to get out of the way of the stench. When she began to walk toward the direction he was sitting, her stomach started to bubble as if she really had a stomach virus.

"I'm sorry for interrupting you, Zack, but I need to run and get some water. Would you like something to drink?" Val said.

Zack knew that he had affected her in some way because he knew he was fine and had a sex appeal that could change any woman's mind about being celibate.

Val ran to the bathroom and began to throw up. After she washed her face, she looked in the mirror and asked herself, "What is wrong with me? I know I am not pregnant because if I were, the child would be four years old by now—that was the last time I had been in contact with a man." Val then went back to her office. "Sorry about the interruption, Zack."

"That's fine, Val. Besides, it's getting late, and I really should be going. It's almost 9:15. I was supposed to be at work an hour ago."

"Well, we didn't get to finish our conversation, but I hope I was able to help you understand why you feel that way," replied Val. "If not, I am truly sorry that I could not help you."

As Zack stood up to put on his jacket, he stretched, and all you could see was his chest and his muscular arms. "Well, I will be back to see you, so that we can finish our conversation."

"Make sure you make an appointment."

"Because of my schedule, I don't know If I could promise a date, so I would rather walk-in. That way, I can squeeze time for my visit."

"That's fine."

Zack looked back at Val before opening the door. "I really wish I could find that one special woman who knows how to take care of me," he said. Then, Zack walked out the door.

Val sat down at her desk and put her hands on her head. "Lord, what just happened? I even forgot to mention you. It's like my mind was distracted. Lord, forgive me. I haven't had a distraction in a while. Lord, please help me. I must be weak somewhere. Lord, I cannot survive or even continue to run my business without you. I need you to strengthen me every minute." She then looked up and said to herself, "I cannot allow my weakness to destroy my salvation."

Val then sat and reviewed over her donations for the month. By then, it was getting closer to 10 A.M. Her appointment would soon be arriving. Charity then buzzed in on Val, letting her know that her next appointment had arrived. It was Allen. "Send him in," Val said.

"Hello, Val," Allen greeted.

"Hello, Allen. Again, I am sorry about Antwan," Val responded. Val then walked toward Allen to give him a hug.

"I have been trying to deal with it, Val, but my flesh wants to have the person who did this found and brought to me personally," Allen said. "I'm starting not to care how old he is."

"Well, you know you can't do that, Allen, because, then, you are not allowing the Lord to work within you."

"Val, to be honest, I am starting to think that the Lord does not care about me, especially for letting this happen. You saw for yourself that my son was attempting to make a change. He had even come to see you on his own."

"I understand you are frustrated," replied Val, "but you are attacking the wrong person. How do you actually know that his visit was intended for a change?"

"Val, please, don't make me walk out on you."

"No! Listen to me, Allen. His visit with me very well could have been his warning from the Lord to change his path before disaster happens. You cannot hate the Lord for the choices your son made."

"That still does not explain why God didn't save him."

"God allowed him to choose his own fate by his decision," explained Val. "Allen, I know what I'm about to say is going to sound strange to you, but Antwan did not allow the Lord to direct his path. Even though he is gone now, I still respect my clients as if they were here in my presence. I told Antwan some things that were clear as day. All he had to do was take heed. It was a warning! His visit is now clear to me. He came here because the Lord told you where to steer him so he could get his warning. Allen, I know things are confusing for you right now, and believe me, that is totally understandable, but you must remember that revenge cannot be yours. Whatever you have or feel in your heart to do will be wrong. You will be making a huge mistake. The person who did this will be punished in his time. He is not going to get away with what he has done."

"What if they never catch the person?" asked Allen, close to tears.

"God was there," Val answered. "He saw who did it, and if man never catches him, he will pay whether it will be next week, next month, or a few years from now. It will come back around."

"That just won't be fast enough for me. They need to suffer now for what they have done. They have taken the only family that meant the most to me—my only child, my son."

"By you staying faithful to the Lord and trusting him to heal your pain, he will give you something back."

"I don't want to start over with another kid. I don't think the Lord could ever give me something more precious than my boy."

"Allen, listen to what you are saying," replied Valoria. "Do you not think if the Lord gave you your son that he could not give you something that you could love just as much as him and even more?"

"I don't know. You don't know what it is like to lose a child, Val. That is a pain that can be so unbearable that it changes your whole demeanor as a person."

"I may not know what it is like to lose a child, but I can assure you that it is not like losing yourself," Val said. "The soul that was born to you has never been yours from the start, but the soul that is in you belongs to you. It is the only one that you can think for, live for, feel for, and take care of all the time. A child is that, it's a child until it is raised to an adult, and after that, it goes out on his or her own to build a life and care for itself. You then, at that point, have no control. You can only talk to, assist financially, and love from a distance. It's no longer your choice on what he or she wants to eat or choose the clothes or decides who they bear children with. That soul is only one you can hope stays on the right path and finds God, as you have for yourself. Everyone will feel deserted at least once in their life when they lose someone extremely close to them, but you must remember that there is only one person who will never die and desert you. He is the only one who has been with you from the beginning and will be with you to the end and thereafter. He is more precious to you than any family member or child you will ever have. He is the one who gives your life to be able to produce other life for him. So, don't be mad at God because, just like your son, you can be gone and not know what's happening to anyone you know. Pray that the Lord have mercy on his soul, but don't envy him. He is a perfect God, whether you want to accept it or not. Just think long and hard before you decide or not."

"Okay, Val, I get the point. I guess I'm just sad and wish I never had to experience anything like that—it is so hard," Allen responded. Allen began to cry. For a few minutes, there was nothing but silence in her office, and then, Allen's phone rang. He answered the call. "Hello!"

It was Detective Wallace. "Hello, Allen."

"Hi, Detective," Allen replied. Allen stood and walked over to the window. He looked at Val as to signal her that he needed a few moments of privacy. So, Val nodded and walked out of her office to Charity's desk. When she walked out of her office; Charity had her back turned with her earpiece on. She did not hear when Val opened the door. Val walked over to her and tapped her on the shoulder. Charity jumped as if she had seen a ghost.

"Thanks for almost giving me a heart attack," Charity said.

"I'm sorry. Allen got an important phone call, so I decided to step out for a moment so he could talk in private," Val replied.

"Now, I am puzzled."

"Why?"

"Because that is your office. If anything, he should have stepped out."

"Well, thanks for the tip, but we were in the middle of a session, and to be honest, how much privacy would he get out here in the lobby? Besides, what were you doing?"

Charity just knew she was caught, so she changed the subject quickly. "Who might that be coming up the elevator?"

"I don't know. Do I have another appointment?" Val asked.

"No, not that I know of," Charity answered.

Then, Val thought about Leia. "I know who it could be," she said. Soon, she started to guess. She stepped off the elevator. It was Leia. Val then walked over to the elevator to greet her and to let her know that she would be with her shortly. "It is so good to see you. I see you are just a few minutes early. I am in the middle of a session, but I will be done soon. Would you like something to drink?" Val said as she approached Leia.

"No, thank you," Leia responded.

"Well, have a seat. Make yourself comfortable, and Charity will keep you company while I finish up."

"Okay, thanks."

Val smiled at Leia and walked back into her office.

Allen had just hung up the phone. He had gone and sat down on the chair and covered his face completely.

"Is everything okay, Allen?" Val asked.

"Actually, everything just got worse. That was Detective Wallace. He was calling to tell me that the person who shot my son has turned himself in."

"That is great, but why are you even more upset than before?"

"Well, the only problem now is, my… he has turned into a she."

"She?" Val asked, confused.

"His ex-girlfriend, Trina," explained Allen. "They have been broke up for about four months now. He had been seeing another girl since her. What's even more devastating is that she is pregnant, and she says Antwan is the father. She told the detectives she called his phone as he was leaving his friend's house and asked if he could give her some money. He told her that he had to go to his mother's house and then he would come by and give her some money. She said she was frustrated and got mad because she felt as if he was going to mistreat her since he had another girlfriend and she was pregnant with his kid. She said she told him if he did not meet her and give her the money, she was going to call and tell me that she was pregnant. He then went ahead and met her around the corner in the alley. She said he told her he was tired of her threatening him with calling me because he thought I would be ashamed, so he said he would call and tell me himself. She said that when he was dialing the number, she asked him why he had not already told me. He told her, 'Because I should have stopped when something told me, too, but you kept on.' She said she then became angry, pulled out her gun, and shot him several times. She said she cut between two houses and went home. She said since she has been at home, she has been having bad dreams. The one that caused her to turn herself in was the one she had last night. She said she dreamed that she had a son, and one day, when she was sleep, he came in her room and choked her to death. She is now in jail, with a five-hundred-thousand-dollar bond. The detective said she does not want to see me even when she goes to court. But when her son is born, she wants me to have him. She said she will sign over all rights to me if I want him."

"So, she is having a son?" asked Val.

"That's another thing, Val. They don't know what sex the baby is yet, and she is only three months pregnant. Val, what if the baby is not Antwan's? How can I commit to taking care of a child who I would not know if it was his or not? I am not prepared to take care of a child. I have had my days of diapers. I don't want any more. I just need to take the day off from work and get my thoughts together. I will make another appointment with Charity, but I must go home now, Val."

"Okay, Allen, please try to relax. Call me if you need me before your next appointment. I am here for you, and I will continue to pray for you," Val replied.

"Thanks," said Allen, "because I need it. I don't think I have the strength to pray for myself right now. Thanks." When Allen walked out of the office, he stopped at Charity's desk so he could make an appointment. Leia was standing at the desk, looking at some pictures that Charity had. "Excuse me?" Allen said to both of the ladies. Leia looked around swiftly.

"Hey, Allen, I'm sorry. You need to make an appointment?" Charity asked.

"Yes, for next Tuesday," Allen responded.

"Okay, I got it," Charity said.

Allen began to walk off, and when he walked past Leia, he said, "How are you?" Then, he continued to walk to the elevator. Leia turned around, looked at Val's door, and noticed her walking toward it. As she walked toward the doorway, she told Leia that she was ready. Leia then proceeded to walk in the office.

"Hello, Leia, I am so glad you were able to make it," Val greeted.

"I'm glad I was able to make it, too," Leia responded.

"How is work?" Val asked.

"It's just work," Leia replied.

"I have a friend in the real estate. I think you should give her a call and just get a little information on how you can get involved in it," said Val. "As a matter of fact, the guy who just left is in the real estate. Maybe I can get him to give me some brochures or some information on it."

"Was that your boyfriend?"

"Oh no," Val replied. "I don't have a boyfriend. I keep my personal life very separate."

"He couldn't have been a client. He does not look like the type who would be seeing a shrink."

"Not everyone has to look a certain way to get counseling. There are so many people like you and him who do not look like they have one problem. Problems do not discriminate. People whom you least expect have problems. That is just something that we cannot escape as humans. Even if we personally do not have a problem, if a close friend or family member goes through tough times, depending on our closeness to them, we will share some of the discomfort they feel," Val explained.

"Is he having problems with his wife or something?" Leia asked.

"Unfortunately, I cannot discuss his or anyone's problem with anyone. It is strictly confidential. But, no, he is not married. You sound as if you are fishing for information."

"No, I'm not. I'm just asking a question."

"Tell me something good," Val said.

"I am just having a problem with my weight. I have been skinny all of my life, but now that I have started my diet, I just cannot stay focused on keeping it up. I want to get all of my hair cut off, but I don't want to be called bald and ugly," Leia said.

"Why do you keep referring to yourself as ugly?" asked Val.

"Because I am," Leia answered seriously. "No one has ever told me I was pretty. I have heard people tell other people around me that they were pretty, but never me. I have had people compliment my outfits, or when I was getting my hair done, they would ask me who done it, but they never say I am pretty."

"I am here to tell you, today, that you are beautiful."

"Val, you are just saying that because you feel obligated to tell me that based on what I just told you."

"No, Leia, I know you wish that was the case, but I'm sorry to disappoint you. The one thing that I am not is shallow. I have had my days of being shallow and judgmental, but since I have been living for God, I view things differently. I see what most people don't see even in themselves. And what I see in you is a beautiful, kindhearted woman who wants to be loved, not only by someone else, but herself as well."

"How do you know?"

"Because you are here," answered Val. "Anytime you seek something better for yourself, you tend to weigh all your options and take chances on things that you think is impossible. By you being here, not knowing why you chose to come, is a sign that you want to change."

"Maybe you are right, maybe you are not. When I talked to you last, you made plenty of sense, so I thought it would not hurt if I come by to give you the opportunity to talk to me. I cannot lose any more than I already have."

"Let me ask you something," Val said.

"What's that?" Leia asked.

"What is your daily routine?"

"Well, when I get off in the morning, I usually go home, make me some breakfast, take a shower, put on my nightclothes, and go to bed like it's late night. I normally wake up around 3 P.M., make me some dinner, and get my clothes ironed for that night, so I can be ready for work. I use to read, but I don't anymore. I just eat and watch TV. That is my weekly routine."

"What about on the weekends?"

"I work overtime, if it is offered, but if not, I just sleep."

"Do you ever go to church?"

"No, I have not been to church since I was a child," said Leia. "To be honest, I don't really get into that. I do believe in God, but I don't pray. I feel like God knows me since he created me, so there is no need for me to pray. He knows everything already."

"Oh, I see. Did you know that God wants a relationship with everyone of us?" said Valoria. "God may know everything, but he still wants you to acknowledge him. I will give you an example. It may not be directly to the point, but you will understand what I am trying to say. It's like a baby who cries for her mother. She knows that her mother is there and knows that her mother knows she has to eat and stay clean. Every need she has, she knows that it has to come from Momma or Daddy, but she cries because she wants to be noticed. You can be looking directly at the baby, and the baby could be looking right back at you and still be hollering. God does not need you because he is the greatest. You need him. And like that baby who cries, you will be tired of just crying, and when you get tired, you will start to reach because you know where your help comes from. I am a woman of God, and I do the works of him. You are that baby; your tears have become dry, so now you are reaching for some guidance—guidance that only God can give. There are so many counselors out here, and you make enough money to pay one, but you choose to come and see me because the good in you has recognized the good in me, and you chose to come here. I am not trying to be demanding or direct you the way I want you to go, but I simply want to allow the Lord to work through me to get to you. When you are through with your sessions with me, it will be up to you to stay on track. You see, Leia I use the word of God to instruct me on how to talk to people and give them advice. Every situation here on earth, God has a word and some instructions on how to achieve eternal life while going through trials and tribulations. No matter how impossible it is for things to get for us, there is nothing too hard for the Lord. We, as humans, can never be too smart or too educated about life to escape the presence of

God. He allows the sun to shine and the moon to burn. The same sun that burned at the beginning of human civilization is still burning today, and the same goes for the moon. Also, you have trees that have been here longer than your great-great-grandparents. Unless you are some of these trees, the moon and the sun, your life is Leia and time is not on your side. Because we, as human beings, come and go like the seasons. Our souls are forever, but our physical lives are not. The life that you live, will determine where your soul lives when your body dies. So, I think now is a better time than ever to drink the milk of life that God has for you."

"I never thought of it that way."

"Most people don't. Our time is running short, but before we end today's session, I want to tell you to go home and write out another routine, but this time, write out the impossible, but you know you can physically do. I want you to follow your schedule, and when you come back, tell me your progress. The reason I want you to do this is because you will notice a change in routine that will mean a change in your life. Include only positive steps," Val instructed.

"It's going to be hard for me to write out a positive routine and actually follow it. Please give me suggestions."

"If you want things to change, you will do it. I cannot tell you what to change because only you know what is comfortable or what works at a slow pace and then gradually builds up. Leia, this is your transformation, not mine. You have to do this for yourself. During your process, I will intercede for you until your vision becomes clear. Another thing I want you to do is pray. Even if you don't know how, now is the time to learn. If you only say three words, say, 'Lord, help me.' You will notice your prayer will start to become more personal. God already knows, but it's time for you to start talking to him and allow him to talk back to you."

"He will talk back?"

"Yes, he will," assured Val. "He will respond to you however your faith speaks to him."

"When should I come back?"

"In two weeks, I think that will be suitable because it might just take you a couple of days to start your routine."

"You really know how to read people, huh?"

"I am not a psychic. I just listen to my heart and give you the best advice that is pleasing to the Lord."

When Leia left, Val took a minute to gather her thoughts. She had to think of a way, should she get some alone time, since it had been about four months since she spent some time alone, to relax her mind and body. Val decided to go home a little early that day. "Charity, do I have any more appointment today?" Val asked.

"No, what's wrong?" Charity replied.

"I'm just little tired today. You know, it has been about eight months since I went home a little early."

Serenity They Seek

"It is about time. You are long overdue for some rest, Val. I know you rest at night when you are at home, but there is nothing like a little daytime sleep."

"You are right," Val agreed, "so I think I am going to take advantage of it. If I have a walk-in, only call me on my cell if it is an emergency."

"I will not! If they have an emergency, I will tell them where the nearest hospital is."

"Ha-ha-ha-ha, you know what I mean, silly."

"Val, just go home and relax. Have some you-time to reflect on your own life," Charity advised.

"Thanks, Char!" Val replied.

"No, Val, thank you!"

As Val was on her way home, she decided to stop at the store to get her son some Jell-O, so she could have it ready for Isaac when he got home from school. While she was in the store, a woman and her husband came in the store together. They were walking in the same aisle as her, and they were talking about what happened last night at the cookout they had. They were laughing and discussing the food items they needed. Val acted as if she was not listening. She picked up her Jell-O and proceeded to the checkout line. By coincidence, the couple was done shopping, so they went to the checkout line, too. They ended up in the long line behind Val, so at this point, she had no choice but to hear any conversation they have. While standing in line, she heard the man tell the woman he would be right back. She looked out of the corner of her eye as the man walked over to the floral section and purchased one pink rose. At that point, it puzzled Val. Why did he not get a red rose? When he returned, the woman was surprised and excited at the same time. Val overheard the woman say, "Honey, we have been married twelve years and you still find ways to show me you love me. What am I going to do with you?" Val wanted to turn around and say, "Awwwww!" But she did not want the couple to know she was listening to everything they were saying. Right as the line was moving, she heard the man say, "Baby, you are still beautiful to me. I'm so glad that I married you." At this time, the line started to move a little quicker.

The woman behind her said to her husband, "Baby, this is the prettiest pink rose I have ever had."

The man responded, "Do you know what it means?"

"No, not really. I do know what the red and the white rose means though," the woman answered.

The man responded, "The pink rose means pure love and the love to come." At that point, Val had reached the checkout, and she was glad. The love between the couple behind her was starting to make her sad because that's how she had imagined her marriage to be with her son's father. Val checked out, and as soon as she got to the car, she began to cry. She said aloud, "Lord, I'm sorry for being so weak when it comes to love. I play this role like I am too strong to have someone in my life. I want you to know, Lord, if you send me a husband, I will accept him, and if I never get married again, I'm asking you to give me peace with being alone. Yours will be done!"

Val got home and began to clean up. She cooked spaghetti and made her son some green Jell-O. It was his favorite. She then took a shower, laid down, and thought herself to sleep. Her son got off the school bus and noticed his mother's car in the driveway. He usually expected his aunt or his babysitter to be there. He was excited, so he rushed home. He had a key, so he came on in the house. "Momma? Where are you?" Isaac called out. Val did not answer because she was lying on her bed in peaceful sleep. She had her alarm set to get up to meet Isaac at the bus stop, but she slept through it. Isaac walked by her room and saw her lying across the bed. He walked over to her and saw she was breathing and that she was just asleep. Isaac then went into the living room and opened up his backpack. He pulled out a picture he drew for her. It was a picture of lilies with the words "I Love you, Mom!" He then took the picture to her room and laid it on her dresser. After doing that, he went to the kitchen and got himself something to drink. He then went back to the living room and turned on the TV. When Isaac turned it on, he accidently turned it up loud. That startled Val, so she jumped up and ran into the living room. She saw Isaac sitting on the couch watching *Spiderman*.

"Isaac, hey sweetie, why didn't you wake me up?" Val said.

"I was at first, Momma, but you looked happy sleeping," Isaac answered.

"Baby, I'm sorry I did not meet you at the bus stop."

"That's okay, Mom. I like walking with Chase and Robert." Chase and Robert were brothers. They lived next door. Val then walked back in her room to straighten up her bed before she got ready for dinner. As she was walking out of her room, she noticed a drawing on her dresser. She picked it up and began to cry again, but this time, silently. She knew, then, she was going to be alone all her life, but she was okay with it because she knew she had God and Isaac.

The next morning, Val arrived at the office surprised to see that Charity had not arrived yet. She normally gets there before her. Val stopped at her desk and logged on to her computer and checked the messages. There was a message from Charlene. She said she would be in today about 12:30 and asked if Charity could let Val know that she would be coming in as a walk-in. Val then got up from Charity's desk and went into her office. She left her door open, so, she could hear and see someone coming in. She decided to wait for at least thirty minutes before she called to see if Charity was all right.

About fifteen minutes had passed and in walked Charity. She came straight to Val's office. "Hey, Val, I am so sorry that I'm late. I got sick early this morning, so I had to go to the emergency room," Charity said.

"Are you okay?" Val asked.

"Yes, I just felt sick," Charity responded.

"You always talk about me, but you may be having morning sickness yourself. Do you think you are pregnant?"

"You almost made me curse just then," replied Charity. "No, I'm cool with the three that I have."

"Do you think you are going to be able to stay at work for the rest of the day?"

"Yeah, Val, I'm fine now."

"Okay, but if you feel yourself getting sick, you can leave."

"Thanks, Val. Oh, by the way, did you get some rest yesterday?"

Val sat down at her desk and said, "I sure did. Thanks for asking."

"Good, you needed it."

"Just so you know, I have already logged on to your computer and checked the messages."

Charlene showed up right on time. "Hello, Charlene," Val greeted.

"Hey Val, been busy today?" Charlene asked.

"Not really, just steady as usual. How are you doing today?"

"I guess I can say I am all right. I just cannot remember the last time I have had a peaceful sleep."

"Really?" Val said. "You know you could have mentioned this a long time ago, Charlene."

"I know, and really, I should have because then I could have dealt with both of my problems at the same time."

"Well, that is not exactly the reason why you could have because, sometimes, it's wise to take your time to work out problems—too much can be destructive," remarked Val. "So it's fine, but I would have just prayed for rest for you. It's still not too late. I am going to pray for rest for you. When I used to go through the same problem, in the mist of my restlessness, I had bad dreams occasionally, so even when I did sleep, I could not rest."

"You have had problems?" Charlene asked.

"Oh, yes, I have been to the trenches, but God kept me safe at my lowest. I then let go and let him pull me out. Slowly but surely, he pulled me out, and I have lived for him ever since. I am so happy. Many people say that no one can be perfectly happy, but that is not true because when you serve God and your heart is pure, as long as you keep your mind stayed on him, he will keep it in perfect peace. This happiness I feel is the happiness that only God can give. Money, fortune, and fame cannot give me this feeling. Everything in this world that makes a person happy is not permanent. Example, if money makes you happy, if you ever lose it, you will not be happy anymore. If you are famous, there will always be someone else becoming famous and sitting in the spotlight seat, so that will then cause you to feel second, when you were once first. You would never be the only one with the gift of music or acting or any other profession you are in that has made you famous," Val explained.

"That's true, Val," agreed Charlene. "Unfortunately, I am not in neither of those categories. What I am having a problem with is my past. I can't let go of the bad choices I once made. I have a lot of regrets."

"I see," said Val. "When do you think about your past the most?"

"When I am alone, driving in my car, or basically, when I have nothing to do, my mind just races backward. I know I have a good job as an accountant, but I feel that if I had done a lot of things differently, I probably would be even more advanced now. I probably would be married with kids. I might just be happy with my life."

"Do you believe you would be happy if you had done everything in that exact order?" Val asked.

"Yeah, and you know, I would have included the Lord," Charlene said.

"Do you think you would have included the Lord if you already were happy with the things you just named first before him?"

"I don't mean it like that, Val."

"I know. I'm just asking."

"Well, yeah."

"I see. I want to tell you about this dream I had before. It was a long time ago, but I can remember it like it was yesterday. It is so clear because I still apply it to my life every day."

"Is it about a real person?"

"I have never seen a face," replied Val. "I just know that the situation is a lesson that we all should learn. It started like this. There was a woman, who was walking in what looked like a mall. I could feel her happiness through my dream; she was humming as she was walking. The song she was humming, as I recall, was 'No Greater Love.' I saw her about to walk around the corner, and right as she turned, she bumped into an old boyfriend. To her, he looked the same. He still dressed and talked the same. She had not seen him in years. When he asked her how she was doing, she told him she was happy, and that she was. She did not worry about anything anymore. She was at peace for the first time in her life. Once, she told him she was living for God and doing all the right things. He laughed as if he was in disbelief. He then proceeded to remind her of who she use to be and all of the things he remembered about her and the things they used to do. When he was done, he congratulated her and walked away. She stood there for a minute and started replaying her past as if it was yesterday. Her past had just bumped into her in the flesh. She was happy about who she was not, but she became ashamed and regretful all over again. She wished she never had met him or did any of the things he reminded her of. When she got home, she sat as if she was still replaying her past, until eventually, guilt, shame, and regret came back into her heart. She then became sad. Then, her sadness turned into depression. She stopped praying, reading her Bible, and going to church. One day, she was driving to work on a rainy Monday morning. Her mind was cloudy all morning because, now, she started to feel bad about not going to church and praying anymore. There was a school bus stopped up ahead on the road she was traveling. By the time she focused on the road ahead, a little child had begun to run across the road to the bus. The woman did not have time to stop, so instead of hitting the child, she swerved and hit a pole. When they found her, she was still alive? She was crying, and right before she was pulled from the car, she cried herself to death.

She died in her tears that wet Monday morning. You see, Charlene, when you let the Lord come into your life, he will clean you up and purify you from everything not of him. Only good thoughts and good decisions should rest among you. When the Lord takes regret from you, it will be up to you to keep it out. The Lord is looking for a pure heart. He does not want to live in your regret when he has forgiven you and removed that from your heart. You can be doing everything else right, but in case you did not know, that small regret that you are holding on to is no different from killing someone. It can cause you to fall even more swiftly than an old habit."

"I did not know that. I may not understand how that can be equal to murder. To me, murder is the worst sin ever."

"No sin is greater than the other."

"I know that, but how is regret a sin?" Charlene asked.

"Because you are saying to God that you don't trust or believe he has delivered you from that. You want to go back and fix it yourself. Regret can cause you to keep a distance from the Lord because you are too ashamed to face him fully, so you stay at a distance and doubt yourself. If God forgives you, who are you not to forgive yourself? You are certainly not greater than he. Anytime you depend on yourself to fix a problem and try to handle an old situation, you are telling God you don't need him."

"Oh, okay, now I see what you are saying. I don't want him to think that."

"So, you know what you are going to have to do then, right?" inquired Val.

"Yeah, I'm going to have to let go of my past and let it be just that, a memory, but I can wish I could change it."

"Right."

"So, if you don't mind me asking you, Val, even when your past crosses your mind, how do you deal with it?"

"It's okay to remember and recapture the images," Val said. "But when you replay it in detail, you tend to let old feelings back in. I have used my past as examples many times, but when I do, I just recapture it and pause the details in my memory, while at the same time thinking about how God spared me every time. And because I have my mind stayed on him at the same time, he overrides what the devil will try to use to corrupt me again."

"So, you are saying that every time I think about something bad, I should think about God at the same time?"

"That's right!" Val pointed out.

"I'll try that, but I don't know how that is going to work."

"Well, then, I want you to do it here, right now, while I am in your presence," Val enthused.

"I can't, Val. I don't have the strength you have. I don't think I can put God in the same category as my past."

"You are missing the point. I'm going to do this. I want you to lie back on the chair for a minute."

So Charlene laid back on the chase. Right then, Charity buzzed in on the intercom. "Val?" Charity asked.

Val picked up the phone and said, "Yes?"

"You have a walk-in who has just came in," Charity said.

"Okay, thanks, tell them I will be done shortly. Thanks for letting me know."

"If you have to go, I can come back later," said Charlene.

"It does not work that way. They will wait patiently, and you are not here to worry about that. Now, what I want you to do is lay back and close your eyes."

"What are you going to do?"

"You will see, just do it." So Charlene closed her eyes and lay back on the chair. "Now, I want you to picture a grey wall or any color you want with nothing on it. When you do this, you clear your thoughts. When I tell you I want you to start thinking about your past, I want you to start with the worst memory, the one that really brings you down the most." Val paused for about thirty seconds and then said, "Start now." Val waited for about one minute, so she could let her get deep in thought, and then, out loud, she began to pray while Charlene was laying there in deep thought. "Lord, I am coming here today, standing in for Charlene. I ask that every memory that she is having right now become just that, a memory with no effects or feelings. I'm asking you to step into her thought where she is and show her you were with her then, that you are the reason she is here today, alive, in good health, and only remembering where she once was. Lord, let her know that the things she went through was a part of her life that she had to experience, so she could become the person she is today and still yet to become. Lord, we so badly wish that we had our own life planned out the way we want it to go. We don't realize that we did not give ourselves life, but we feel as if we can punish ourselves for our bad decisions and our mistakes, which are the unforeseen circumstances that have come in our paths."

While Val was praying, she walked in the direction where the chair was. Then, she immediately stopped praying. When she stopped, Charlene opened her eyes as if the music she was listening to had stopped. "Why did you open your eyes, Charlene?" Val asked.

"I heard you stop praying!" Charlene said.

"So, when I stopped praying, you stopped thinking?"

"No, I stopped thinking when you start praying." Charlene said and sat straight up in the chair. "That was weird."

"What happened was my prayer, out loud, overpowered the regretful thoughts in your head," explained Val. "You could no longer concentrate on that because the power of the Lord is much greater than any and everything here on Earth, even your thoughts. I'm going to give you a word of advice, and then I am going to end our session for today. Every time your past comes in your mind, even in the middle of your sleep, if you feel that you just can't pray, just keep saying Jesus until you see that blank-colored wall that you saw today when you cleared your mind."

"Thanks, Val, I will call and make an appointment with Charity. You are the wisest person I know!"

"Not wiser than Solomon!"

"Who is Solomon?" Charlene asked.

"A king in the Old Testament whom God blessed with wisdom that no other man has ever had," Val answered. Charlene had no idea that Val was directing her to the word so that she can get a better understanding and begin to seek and find the Lord herself. Charlene left Val's office, thinking about Solomon in the Old Testament. Val was hoping that she would go home and read it, for if she did, her interest would grow more, and she would seek and definitely find all of answers to her questions.

Val buzzed Charity. "Yes, Val?" Charity answered.

"Is my walk-in still out there?" Val asked.

"Yes, are you ready?" Charity said.

"Send them in exactly three minutes," Val instructed.

Val sat at her desk and typed in her laptop a few notes from her visit. Three minutes had passed and in walked a young lady. Val stood and said, "Hello, my name is Valoria. I'm sorry I did not ask Charity what your name was."

"Hi, my name is Keasha," the young lady responded. She was very pretty, but she looked to be as if she was only about nineteen years old. She had on a Baby Phat jumpsuit, and she had her hair done up like the young teenagers are wearing their hairs today. Val looked at her clock on the wall as she walked over to close her laptop. She noticed that time was really trying to get away from her, not that it mattered, but she normally liked to have at least an hour before close time to update her notes, so she would not have to take it home. Val knew by the girl being a little young, she would have to relax and almost come down to her level to make her feel comfortable, so Val took a seat on her desk.

"Have a seat, Keasha. How can I help you today?" Val asked.

Keasha was shy and very scared. She kept fiddling with her hands as if she was extremely nervous. "I have never been to a shrink before. My big sister told me about you. She said she had been here to see you before, a long time ago. She told me that you talk about God a lot," Keasha said. Then she stopped talking, looked down, and started to cry. Val just let her cry. She had learned over the years that when people cry, you have to let them because when you comfort a client physically, you can become emotionally involved. The only one who can take on all of the world's emotions is God.

"Talk to me, sweetie," Val said.

"I want to start to go to church, but I am confused about what church is right. I have been doing a lot of things that are wrong and I am feeling bad about it. I don't want to be a bad person anymore," Keasha confided.

"What makes you feel that you are a bad person?"

"I don't know. I just feel like that," said the young woman.

"The reason I have to ask, Keasha, is so that I will know how to address you and give you the best advice possible," Val explained to her latest client. "I know you have not been here before, and you feel uncomfortable talking to a complete stranger. I want you to know that I am not going to tell anyone your business. I am here to help you, not hurt you. I don't know if you have ever heard of what a shrink does, but I am not like what you have heard. I use my work to give you the best possible advice with the word of God. I don't give out medication or diagnose you with my theory of your life. No matter how much people have a similar situation, we all are very different. You came here because somewhere in your heart, you have faith that coming to see me would help you somehow. The majority of people who come to see me know that I talk about the Lord and, somehow, I believe they know that they will get some advice that they can use to make them a better person. I'm asking you, Keasha, to try to be yourself, open up, and talk to me like I am your friend. If you feel more comfortable, you can lie down and close your eyes. For some people, it helps them focus on their problem, and it takes their mind off me looking at them."

"Okay," Keasha answered. She laid back on the chair, took a deep breath, and began to talk. "I lost my virginity early. I have been with a lot of guys. I have ruined my reputation. There are rumors that I am a freak, and I am tired of being teased. Every time I get a boyfriend, that is all he wants to do."

"Don't take this the wrong way, but why do you do it?" Val asked.

"I don't know—because I am stupid. I don't know. Sometimes, I don't care anymore because I have already messed my life up," Keasha replied.

"Do you ever make that choice because you want to?"

"Sometimes."

"Why do you feel you have messed up your life?"

"Because I have…I have a reputation."

"So, you feel that because you have a reputation, your life is over?"

"Yep," Keasha said. "Even though I don't have any kids, and I don't have any diseases. But even though I have been to the doctors and they tell me I don't have AIDS right now, I have heard it can take up to ten years before it shows up."

"You have been educated by man, so now let me educate you by God. First, let me ask you, do you believe in Jesus?"

"Yes."

"Okay, if you don't mind me asking you, how old are you?"

"Twenty," Keasha answered.

Val decided that she would start off slow, by her being a young girl who already feels left behind. She wanted her to slowly grasp the conversation. She knew that by the time she left her office, she would be a woman. "Keasha, the story I am about to tell you is about a lady in the Bible. This not referred to you, but the situation is very similar. There was a lady, by the name of Mary. She was a very promiscuous woman. One day, she was cornered by some men and women in her town. They were all surrounding her, calling her names, and wanted to kill her for the way she was. Jesus showed up and saved her. The woman was very scared. She felt deserted and alone. Jesus told the men and women who wanted her dead that whoever has no sin, cast the first stone. No one there could throw a stone. Jesus then told the woman to go and sin no more. That day changed the woman's life forever. Now, the people of her village remind me of the people who are talking about you and spreading rumors about you. Their harsh words are the stones that they threaten you with. People who sit around, talk about people, and help contribute to rumors are typical wrongdoers. Most of them hide behind someone else's faults to keep from having to deal with their own. Others have changed and feel they are better than those who still do wrong, so to make their change stand out more, they magnify others' mistakes so they stand out to be recognized. The only thing the changed ones don't realize is that they have changed for the worse. Instead of tearing down, they have a tool to build up. So where they think they are better, they are actually worse than they were when they were out there. They did not have a tool then, so they could not help the weak. Do you understand?"

"Yes, Ma'am," Keasha responded.

"As far as diseases are concerned, when you allow God to come into your life, wholeheartedly, he will cure you of anything you feel that is impossible. He will wipe your body and your health clean."

"How will I know if I have done it wholeheartedly?" asked Keasha.

"Unfortunately, you won't. You just have to breathe, talk, walk, and think like Jesus."

"I don't know where to begin, though."

"I know that it is easier said than done. You see, when you pray for healing, you can't ask with a doubtful heart. You can pray for something, but if deep down, you still have doubt that it can happen the way that you pray for it, then it really won't. But if you believe in your heart that no matter how hard it looks that it will happen, then it will. Keasha, you first have to build up your faith and relationship with God."

"How do I do that?"

"Well, you have to start by praying. Do you know how to pray?"

"A little," said the young lady.

"After you pray, pick up your Bible and read a verse. As you begin to pray and read, you will begin to want to know a little bit more every day. Now, I do want to tell you that once you start to do this, there are going to be other options coming to you that may seem to be better than the one that you are choosing. There will be guys who will begin to come to you, talking a whole new conversation. You must avoid them. They do not mean what they say. It is a distraction to keep you from seeking the Lord. Do you have a Bible?"

"No, but my mother does."

Val then walked over to her desk and pulled out one of her personal Bibles. She removed her bookmark, walked over to Keasha, and handed it to her.

Keasha looked up at Val and said, "Thank you, but you don't have to give me your Bible."

"Well, do you want to go with me to buy you one?" Val offered.

"No," Keasha declined.

"Okay, then accept this one. I can't give you advice and you don't have the resource you need."

"I do have a job. I could have gone and bought me a Bible."

"Would you?" Val asked, looking intently at her client.

"I don't know."

"I normally leave it up to my client to come back and see me, but I want to see you in two weeks, if your schedule permits."

"What day?"

"At your convenience, but it must be in two weeks. Of course, if you need to see me sooner, you may come any time during business hours. There will be something I will have to tell you then."

"How come you can't tell me now?"

"Because I don't know what it is yet," answered Val.

Keasha looked at Val with a puzzled look and said, "Okay, I can come on my day off, which is on a Wednesday."

"Okay, that's fine."

Keasha left, and Val gathered her things to leave for the day. Right before leaving, she stopped and talked to Charity for a minute. Charity normally leaves an hour after Val, but that visit lasted a little longer than Val expected, so Charity only had about fifteen minutes left of her day. When Val was getting in her car, her cell phone rang. It was her brother, Mike, calling from Detroit, Michigan.

"Hey, Val," Mike said.

"Hey, Mike! How are things going with you?" Val responded.

"Great! The kids are really growing. How is little Isaac?"

"He is fine. He is the man of the house, so he acts like he has to protect me all the time."

"That's good. Look, the reason I called was to let you know about the convention this year. I know you are busy, but there is a whole lot going on this year that I think you will really enjoy. I think it would be nice for you and little sister to come. Since it is going to be here in Detroit, all of you can stay with me. I really want you to come," Mike invited.

"I really can't make you any promises. I will try to come, though. I was planning on taking a vacation in the upcoming months anyway, so I'll see," Val said.

"Okay, but I want you to try harder than you normally would. I really would like for you to teach a class this year."

"I'll think about it, okay?" Val promised. "I'll talk to you a little later."

The next morning, when Val arrived at work, she noticed Charity had not arrived first again, but this time, she did not check the messages or logged on to her computer because she assumed, she was running a little late like the last

Serenity They Seek

time. Val went into her office and began to type on her laptop the notes that she could not finish yesterday. One hour had passed, but Charity had still not arrived. Val then knew something was wrong. She went to Charity's desk to check the messages to see if she had left a message saying that she would be late. After checking the messages, she did not get one from Charity. She then called her cell from the office, but her phone was powered off. Val then became worried that something had happened. She called Charity's sister, Christy. Christy told Val that Charity was in the hospital. Val then put a note on the door when she would return, locked the glass double doors, and went to the hospital. When she arrived at the hospital, she located Charity.

"Val, how did you know I was here?" Charity asked, surprised.

"I called your sister after one hour had passed to see if you were okay," Val said.

"She was supposed to call you two hours before the day started to let you know that I would not be in today," Charity said, then she began to cry.

"It's okay. I came right away because I did not know what had happened to you."

Charity then just stared at Val as if she was preparing herself for what she was about to tell her. Then, she did it. "I have AIDS, Val," Charity revealed.

Val sat down in the chair beside her and grabbed her hand. "I see...," Val said.

"I have known for about two years now. I never wanted to tell you because I thought you would treat me differently or be afraid to touch me or be around me. That's why when I started, I did not care what anyone thought about me because I am already dead. I am sorry, Val! Because of you, I feel all right about it now. I know that I am not dead yet, but I would have been if I continued to be the person I was. I have changed so much for the good, Val. There is so much that I have not told you. Val, please don't be mad at me for keeping this from you."

"No way am I mad. You felt today was the day to tell me, and that's okay. Lots of people open up on their own timing. I am in no way mad at you. Do you need the rest of the week off?"

"Val, I'm fine. It's just that I can't fight off common colds, so to be on the safe side and to try to stay alive for as long as possible for my kids' sake, I checked myself in."

"I see."

"I'm okay, Val. I have not lost any weight. I am just being extra cautious." Val then reached over and gave her a hug. She stood up and told her she expected her to be at work tomorrow morning, on time. She then smiled and walked out the door. "Hey, Val?" Charity said. Val looked back at Charity. "Thanks for understanding."

"Always! If there is anything I can do, you have every number I own," Val said. She winked and walked out of the door.

Val then went back to the office. When she arrived in the parking garage and got out of her car, as she was walking to the elevator, she noticed Charles standing and waiting for the elevator. "Hello, Charles," Val greeted.

"Hello, Val, I was on my way up to your office to see you for a minute," Charles responded.

"Okay, I'm headed that way, so come on up," Val said. "How is it going with your job search?"

"That's what I was coming to talk to you about."

"Is everything okay?" Val asked.

"Everything is going better than okay," Charles replied. "I want to say thank you for helping me. I got a job about two weeks after I came to see you. I went into the office about three days after my visit with you, and when I was talking to the lady who normally talks to me, that lady named Elizabeth came and got me. She took me into her office instead. She asked me a few questions about myself and asked me if I would be interested in a welding position. I told her that I had never welded before, but I would learn. She made a phone call while I was sitting there and told the person on the other line that she was sending me over. She gave me directions to this metal plant. I went and talked to a guy named James. He showed me around the plant, had a short interview with me, and told me that if I was interested, he would make sure I get the proper training. Val, I started work that following Monday. They started me off at 16.00 dollars with no experience. If it was not for you, I would not have gotten the job."

"No, Charles, if it was not for the Lord, you would not have gotten the job," said Val. "I only called Elizabeth and told her about you, and if she could find someone who would at least give you an interview. God did the rest. I could see the persistence in your change. You really wanted to do the right thing. If everyone who could help someone, they knew was trying to do the right thing, there would be so many people who would see how God works for the good in them. Even though Elizabeth was able to set up the interview, she also was not the reason you got the job. The man could have turned you down, but because God so loves and cares about you, he made the man have a soft heart and not care about your past."

"You are right, and I understand," Charles said.

"Even though you were getting discouraged, you did not give up and head back to the streets."

"What can I say?"

"It's nothing you can say to me, but you can tell the Lord how much you appreciate what he has done for you."

"I am going to do that."

"Charles, you know there is so much more the Lord can do for you to keep that smile on your face, if you let him."

"Well, I certainly won't stop him. How could I not let him?"

"By not doing what he wants you to do," Val answered.

"What does he want me to do?"

Serenity They Seek

"Do you know how to pray?"

"Yes, I did it every night when I was locked up."

"Well, you can ask him yourself. Charles, start praying again like you did when you were in prison," Val explained. "And as you pray, put your heart in it a little bit more each day. As your prayer becomes stronger, you will start wanting to be closer and closer to him because unlike physical human friends, he will be the only one who will never change or go away. I want you to always remember that!"

While she was talking to Charles, the phone was ringing off the hook. Charles said, "Well, I see you are getting really busy. I just wanted to come by in person and thank you for helping me. You told me something that really touched me. I promise I am going to try to apply everything you told me to my life, each and every day."

"Well, good. It was nice to see you again, Charles. I think you are going to be fine," Val said. When Charles left, Val went out to Charity's desk to answer the phone and waited for the mailman. While Val was sitting there, she began to think about Charity. She then began to pray silently for her. The mailman had arrived, and Val got another surprise that she was not expecting. It was a letter from Tamya, the girl who had three kids and was having a hard time dealing with her habits. Val was amazed because she had never gotten a handwritten letter from a client before. She got thank you cards and box candies, but never a handwritten letter. Val opened up the letter and began to read. The letter read:

Dear Valoria Thomas,

I hope you remember who I am, but just in case you don't, I am the lady who came to see you a while ago. I had on a purple and orange toboggan outfit. A lady from the unemployment office called me the day after I left your office. I haven't been to the unemployment office, and I don't have any friends who would look out for me like that, so I figured it could be no one but you at the time who gave her my number. I did have an appointment with her, but my car broke down the day before I was supposed to go see her. Unfortunately, I was unable to make it, and at this time, I still don't have a job. I want to thank you for what you did for my kids. I have never seen their faces so bright. Thank you for the money you sent me. I was able to buy plenty of groceries and pay my rent. Thank you for helping me. I have never met a complete stranger who would extend a helping hand. I must say that you truly are a woman of God. You made a great impact in my life. I did what you said, and I am proud to say that I have been doing it every day. My kids are starting to love me more. Since that day, I have not done any cocaine. I smoked weed twice though, but I am still proud of myself because it could be worse. I know that it is a process. Each day I wake up is a second chance for me. I have been reading that Scripture to me and my kids. They like it very much. I have managed to cut off two of my male friends. There is one left who I am hoping and praying for the strength to let him go. I want you to keep me in your prayers because I think that if someone else prays with me for me, I will see the light. I am so glad I met you, Valoria. I am going to call Elizabeth back and try to schedule another appointment with her. Thank you so much. You are a good person.

    Sincerely,
    Tamya Jones

    Val was touched by the letter. She then took the letter in her office and put it in her folder where her other cards from other clients were. The entire day, while running the office alone, Val had only seen three people. Val was glad it was not very busy.

    The day was over, and it was time for Val to go home. She looked at her schedule for tomorrow. There were only two names on the schedule: Leia and Allen. Val went home and enjoyed her evening with her son.

    When Val got up the next morning, she looked at her calendar to mark down when the convention was being held. Val was thinking about taking her vacation and going to the convention, but she knew that because of Charity's illness, there would be no guarantee that she would be able to stay away from the office for a week. Charity could get sick at any time. While thinking about that, she then changed her way of thinking. She knew that she could not doubt God in any way. When she arrived at the office, Charity was already there. "Good morning!" Val greeted.

    "Good morning, Val. I even came in thirty minutes earlier to make up for the time I was out yesterday," Charity responded.

    "You did not have to do that and you know it," Val said. They both began to laugh. "Charity, I have decided when I want to take my vacation."

    "Good," Charity replied.

    "The one thing that I am not going to do is treat you differently, Charity, so please don't stop being the happy, wonderful person you are."

    "Val, can I ask you a stupid question?" Charity asked.

    "No question is stupid."

    "Are you still going to be comfortable with me bringing you food from time to time when I go and grab something to eat on the days you can't leave?"

    "That was a stupid question, Charity. Yes, I will still trust you. I'm not worried about you or your situation at all. Even if you tried to harm me, you couldn't."

    "And why would you say that?"

    "Because God would not let you," replied Val sincerely.

    Charity looked at her and smiled. "That is the reason I love and admire you so much, Val," Charity said.

    "I admire you, too, Charity. You have more courage and strength than I gave you credit for." Val then smiled and walked into her office to prepare for her two clients for the day.

    Leia was on her way to Val's office. When she stopped at the stoplight, a black Camry pulled beside her. It was Allen. She stared at him as if she wished she could be in his passenger seat; she thought he was so handsome. Leia thought, *I don't know him well enough to get his attention. Besides, he would not recognize me anyway.* She wondered why he was going to see Val for. While she was in deep thought looking toward his car, Allen looked over and saw her looking. Leia suddenly turned away. Before he could remember where he had seen that woman, the car behind him blew the horn to notify him that the light had turned green. Leia finally arrived at Val's office. When Leia came into the office, she noticed that Leia's physical appearance looked the same, but that did not mean anything yet because Val always said that when change starts, it starts from within and the rest would soon follow. Val was sure that Leia had at least done as she instructed her to do and started a list.

"Hello, Val," Leia greeted.

"Hi, Leia, how are you doing?" Val asked.

"I am doing fine. I feel a little better," Leia said.

"Did you start a list?"

"Yes, actually, I did, and like you said, it has taken me about three days to start it. Would you like to see it? I brought it with me."

"That is good that you take it with you wherever you go. That way, you are always reminded of your goals," said Val. "But no, I would not like to see it, and not because I don't want to, but because sometimes we need to keep something for ourselves. That helps us build a strong love for ourselves. We will appreciate our success without anyone's input."

"I understand. I know you said to put the impossible that I know I could do if I put my mind to it on the list, but I also decided to put some goals in there that I could not do, if I wanted to."

"Why do you feel that you could not do it if you put your mind to it?" Val asked.

"Because I will never be as pretty as I want to be," Leia answered.

"Yes, you can, and even more than you imagine."

"Why lie to me, Val?" Leia asked. "I can never change my physical appearance without surgery."

"You are wrong. Anything is possible. The impossible can be made possible if you believe, Leia!" Val insisted. "You can be more than what you desire without surgery, makeup, and jewelry. All of the things I just named are enhancers. They don't make you over because if you remove those things, the real you have to shine. Focus on your dream. Believe and know God will give you what you really want, and watch him give you more than what you asked for. Let me ask you something."

"Sure."

"Out of everything on your list, what percentage do you feel you will accomplish?"

"I'm going to say about 80 percent."

"So, I take it that the things that you don't believe you could do if you wanted to would be the other 20 percent?"

"Yes."

"So, I tell you what, since they will be the hardest to accomplish and will keep you from getting 100 percent, why don't you work on those first?"

"I don't know, Val," said Leia doubtfully. "If I did that, it will take longer for me to get through my list."

"But ask yourself, is it worth it? Ask yourself what is most important to you: the easy tasks or the hardest ones?" asked Val. "The 20 percent you put in there must be. The reason I say that is because you put them in there because they are also what your heart desires."

"I never thought of it that way. I guess you are right because the ones that I know I can't change are the hardest but most desired in my life."

Val and Leia continued to talk for a while. When Leia's session was over, she left, and before leaving, she scheduled another appointment. When Leia was getting off the elevator, she began to cry because, as much as she wanted to believe her life could really change, she doubted it would even happen. She felt good just knowing the thought had even entered her heart. That was the most positive thing that she had done since she graduated from college.

The day was about over. Val was preparing to end her day. "Val, you have a very important phone call," Charity said.

"Okay, send it through," Val replied. Val had always told Charity to treat everyone equally with the same importance, whether rich or poor; they all are human beings with different souls. "This is Valoria," Val answered the call.

"Hello, Ms. Valoria, my name is Sharron Peirce Alexander. I'm not sure if you have heard of me before," the caller answered.

Val knew who she was from a previous movie she had watched. "I know who you are. How are you doing?" Val responded.

"I guess I have had better days," replied the woman. "I heard about you through this man whom I know. He is from your area. He told me that you have helped so many people. I already have a personal shrink whom I have been dealing with, and I have been seeing her for four years. I really will not be able to come and talk to you in person because of my schedule. I was wondering if I could schedule an appointment with you tomorrow over the phone."

"What time would you like to call me?"

"About this time, if possible."

"I don't see where that would be a problem. I normally prepare for the next day the last hour of my day, so I think I can swing that."

"Are you sure?" asked Sharron. "I do not want to inconvenience you because I know how schedules can put you behind. If it is okay with you, I would like to have my accountant call you and settle any charges up front."

"No need, I don't have any fees or charges," replied Val. "But I would like to have my secretary fax you a consent form to sign."

"Look, you don't have to give me anything free because I am a celebrity."

"Ms. or Mrs.?" Val asked.

"Ms," Sharron replied.

"Ms. Alexander, my services are free to everyone."

"Oh, I see. I don't even want to know how you make a living. Trust me, we all have a way of making ends meet, but anyhow, thank for your time. I will talk to you tomorrow around this time."

When they hung up the phone, Val went out to Charity so she could put her on the schedule for a phone session. "Soon, you will be counseling the whole world," Charity jested.

"That is not my intention. I am one person and one person only, and besides, not everyone will want to hear what I have to say. I know you remember some people leaving out of here never to return," Val said.

"Yeah, but to be honest, I don't think they were really looking to be helped."

"Who knows?" asked Val. The day was over, and Val went home and decided to work on the material for the class she decided she was going to teach at the convention. She was trying to figure out what it was she was going to teach about that the women had possibly not heard before. While she was sitting with her pencil in her mouth, the title of her message popped in her head. She instantly knew what she would teach on. The title was "Dress Up for Your Lifestyle."

The next day, Val arrived in her office. One of her clients was already there waiting for her. It was the young girl, Keasha, from a week ago. When her session was over, the girl left with a smile on her face. As soon as she left, Val went into her office to update her notes on the young girl, when Charity buzzed in and said, "You have a walk-in."

"What is her name?" Val asked.

"His name is Clint," Charity said, then whispered, "he has a rainbow bracelet on."

"Send him in, silly," Val said. When Clint walked in her office, she was amazed on how he had this sincere look on his face, as though he just had the worst experience of his life. He was a biracial man with very keen features. His hair was curly. He had a sweater tied around his neck. His makeup was flawless. "Hello, Clint," Val greeted.

"Hello," Clint replied.

"Have a seat. What can I do for you today?"

"I know this is going to sound weird, but I don't want to like men anymore. I have never told anyone. This is the life I have always known. I have never been with a woman before," Clint confided.

"When you say you don't want to like men anymore, where does this want come from?" Val asked.

"What do you mean?" asked Clint, confused.

"Sorry for not making myself clear, but what I mean is, does it come from your mind or your heart?"

"Oh my, slow down for a minute, let me tell you why I feel like this first. You are very straight to the point, or is this how it is when you go see a shrink?"

"I'm sorry if I offended you," replied Val. "Let me tell you how this works. Because my services are different from any other service, I run things a little differently. A lot of times, I don't feel the need to have to know your entire past because, to me, that is your past with an unchanging ground. I like to focus solely on your present and future. I know that your past may have caused what is going on in your life, but something that is in your present is causing you to continue to hold on to what has come and gone. I want you to feel as comfortable as you like, to start wherever you like, but always know that I cannot give you advice on things that has happened years ago. I can only help you for today and tomorrow."

"Oh, okay, I understand. Well, in that case, I think it is coming from both my mind and my heart."

"Okay, could you tell me when did you start having this feeling?" Val asked, continuing with her counseling.

"Well, I actually started having this feeling last week, when me and my boyfriend, Derrick, broke up. It seems that every time I have a bad relationship with a man, I just wish I was not like this. I am so tired of being lied to and cheated on. I used to wonder: would my life be different if I had chosen to be with a woman? Then again, I don't know if I could deal with the blood and stuff. Yuck!"

"When you get these feelings after a breakup, do they go away?" asked Val. "And if so, how long does it take for it to fade?"

"Yeah, it goes away in about a week or two, or until I find someone new. Hell, who am I kidding? I'll never stop loving men." Clint began to cry. "Men, to me, are like a good meal. I crave them and love them so."

"When the feeling goes away after a week or two, does it come back at any time during your contentment?"

"It has once or twice, but something has to always be going wrong for me to really focus on it," answered Clint.

"So, without you taking me the wrong way, I just need to know how to respond to you. What is it that you wanted me to counsel you on today?"

"I'm not sure. I think I am just mad right now, but if you could help me and tell me what you think…?"

"I want you to understand that I am going to be totally honest with you," Val said. "I can't promise you are going to like everything that I say, but it will be the truth without downing you or putting you into a category."

"Go ahead. I'm sure it's nothing I have never heard before with gay bashing."

"No, I do not do such things," replied Valoria. "It's wrong to bash anyone. I would just prefer to pray for you or help you before I talk about you. Clint, homosexuality is one of the hardest things to break free from, but if it is something that your heart truly desires, I know that there is nothing too hard for God to tear out of your life. It sounds to me that you have some regrets that you are unsure about. It sounds like you are feeling bad, but you really don't know why, and that is because you are confused about who you are. You see your life being another way, occasionally wondering what it would have been like if you had chosen another path. On the other hand, you have this life that you live that has not worked out for you. You can't seem to find any peace with anyone. To be honest, it does not matter how hard you try. You are not going to find happiness until you find you. When you do find you, it must be real love and truth. Now, I know you say you have never been with a woman, and it disgusts you just thinking about it, but believe it or not, it is truth. The truth is, you are a giver, and the woman is the receiver. You can compare it to many ways, but you can't have one without the other. Black, white, odd, even, plus, minus, in, out, we can come up with so many examples of opposites, but without it, we all die off. There will only be so much that a man can keep giving you because you can only give so much back yourself, and after a while, you both are going to be full and there will be no more room to give. That's when he will move on to the next."

"Men cheat on women the same way and move on," Clint retorted. "It's all the same."

"Yes, it can be the same," agreed Val, "but the difference is that women and men can at least make a child, something that will link their past and even show proof of their relationship. As far as comparison to relationship, it is totally different. If you compared heterosexual relationships against gay relationships, you will see that it could not compare. Relationships of the opposite sex are more stable and have better-ending results than a gay relationship."

"Is this all about having kids and being with someone for a long time?"

"No, I'm just giving you the truth," Val responded. "I am not trying to persuade you to go and sleep with a woman. All I am saying is that if you truly desire to stop seeing men, it is very important for you to do it as soon as possible and mean it. To me, you are wanting something different, but you are fighting against what's right. Clint, I want you to read this Scripture, which I am about to give you, and if you still feel the same way you do today, I want you to begin to pray with sincerity and sureness in your heart."

"Whatever," Clint said. At this point, he was getting very anxious to leave. He knew that Val had come to him differently than he had ever been approached. He went to church from time to time, so he did not have a problem with her talking about God and the Bible. Val went to her desk, pulled out a note card, and gave it to Clint. "I will read this, and thank you for your time," Clint said. Clint then turned and walked out of her office.

When he closed the door, Val began to say a prayer for him, saying, "Lord, I don't know how much knowledge he lacks, but I am asking you to give him an instant understanding as soon as he reads Romans 1, the entire chapter." Val then went back to her desk, sat there, and finished updating her notes. Val was able to catch up on everything because the phone did not even ring. Charity stepped in and let her know that she was going to lunch, and that she was going to forward all of the phone calls back to her office. As soon as Charity got on the elevator, Val's phone rang. Val answered the phone, "This is Valoria."

"Hello, may I speak with a Valoria Thomas?" the man on the other line said.

"Speaking."

"Hello, my name is Greg Patton. I am an attorney, and I called to get your mailing address." Valoria was very puzzled at this point. She kindly gave the man the address. She knew if she asked questions, it would worry her. She refused to allow worrying to become a part of her life again. "Thanks, you are going to be receiving some papers in the mail. I would appreciate it if you would sign them and send them back promptly."

"After I review whatever it is you send, I shall then have my lawyer review them before I send them back."

"That's fine. Goodbye."

Val hung up the phone and sat there, not believing what had just happened. She stopped everything she was doing and started to pray, that the Lord would give her a calm thought. When she was done praying, she called her lawyer to alert her of the phone call she had just received, so she could be ready to review the paperwork that the man spoke of. Charity had just got back from lunch, but unfortunately, she did not get off the elevator by herself. Val's sister came up there to surprise her by bringing her lunch. It caused Val to not think about the phone call. The Lord had answered her prayer that quickly and gave her a calm thought.

The time was getting close to her phone session. Val checked to see if Sharron signed and sent back the consent form. She had indeed faxed it back. The time had come for her to receive her call. Suddenly, Val's phone rang. "Hello, this is Valoria," Val answered the call.

"Hello, I'm right on time," Sharron said.

"Yes, you are," said Val. "We can start whenever you feel comfortable."

"Okay, I'm ready," replied Sharron. "I, first, would like to say that I choose not to be interrupted with questions. If you don't mind, I would like to finish talking first because I am easily distracted. Sometimes, I get frustrated and will end a session until the next one."

"I understand," Val responded. "Whatever is comfortable for you. I do want to let you know that my goal is to complete one problem at a time. I feel that as long as you let a problem linger, it takes ten times as long to solve it each day it goes unanswered, and by the time you get through that one, the other one is already advanced. Because of its advancement, you are unable to see the results and breathe from the last one. Start when you are ready."

"I have been feeling really depressed and unhappy about my life," started Sharron. "I have money and plenty of activities to keep me busy, but I still feel lonely. I have a boyfriend, but he can't make this lonely feeling go away. My shrink has me on three different medications, and I am still depressed. I think I know why it started. I think when a part of my past surfaced and everyone found out about it, I think that is when I was devastated. I'm still not sure. I am a social drinker from time to time, but because of the medications, I can't really drink. Okay, you can talk now." Sharon was talking really fast. You could hear the frustration in her voice.

"So, you say you have everything that you could and would possibly want?" Val asked.

"Yes, what else?" Val could easily see that even though Sharron had everything she could possibly want, there was still something missing that no amount of money or fame could give her, and that was happiness.

"Do you go to church?"

"No, I have my doubts," replied Sharron. "I don't want to hear about God."

"It is as clear to me as day. You long for something that only he can give you."

"I just told you that I don't want to hear about God. I get it now. That's why your services are free—because you are trying to trap people."

"I'm sorry you feel that way, but I can only speak the truth. There is no medication or peaceful island that can give you what you want."

"You are a real character," said Sharron vehemently.

"I am a character who lives by the very advice that I give," Val responded. "I don't know what you want me to tell you, but I can only tell you the truth. You have even said so yourself, that your medication does not make you feel better. That is because the medication can only suppress your problem, which will soon develop into oppression which causes depression. If you put on white clothes and get a plastic bag, fill it with black ink and squeeze the bag until it burst all on your white suit, how would that make you feel? When all you had to do was not to squeeze the bag. Problems will come and go, but we do not have to let it build up pressure to burst. The only one who can help us control the pressure is God." As soon as Val said that, she heard Sharron hang up the phone. Val sat there, waiting to see if she was going to call back. Twenty minutes had passed, but Sharron still did not call back. Val knew that even though the conversation with her was incomplete, she knew that she heard everything she had said to her. Val then gathered her things and left for the day.

That day had truly been a tiring day for her. When Val got home, Isaac was sitting in front of the TV, playing his football game. Normally, Val would go into her room, put down her things, and prepare for dinner, but today, she decided to do something different because she was ready for a change. So, she ordered pizza, went into the living room, and began to play the game with Isaac.

"Hey, Momma, how was your day?" Isaac asked.

"It was okay. How was yours?" Val answered.

"Hard," Isaac replied.

"Really? Why?"

"Because today was tell-us-about-your-family day," answered Isaac.

"What is wrong with that?"

"Well, because most of the class talked about having both parents in their home. Some of them even have stepparents."

"Isaac, I know that at least three of the children live in a single-parent home," Val said.

"Yeah, and I was one of them. The other kids who live in single-parent homes have other brothers and sisters though, so it doesn't seem as empty."

"Do you think our home is empty without other kids or your father here with us?"

"I'm not saying that, Momma. I just want you to be happy."

"What makes you think I am not happy with just the two of us?"

"I know you have God and you are happy with who you are, but I can feel your loneliness sometimes."

"Boy, you are just ten years old. What do you know about feeling someone else's loneliness?"

"Momma, you are sitting here trying to play my game, messing me up."

Val and Isaac laughed together.

It was now Friday at the office. Val had woken up extremely happy this morning. She had no idea that she was going to receive the package that the lawyer told her she would. Val was sitting in her office, balancing out the monthly bills for the month. Charity came into Val's office.

"Hey, Val, you have a package from DHL delivery service," Charity said. Val was not familiar with that delivery service because all the packages she received came through UPS or FedEx. She knew this had to be an unexpected surprise. She looked at who it was from, and she remembered the name of the lawyer's office that had called her. Val opened the package and began to read. As she was reading, her eyes filled up with tears, and she began to cry softly. There was an insurance claim form that had been issued to her for 350,000 dollars by Ideila Thompson, who was now deceased. She did not recognize the name so she continued to read each page. She came to a page that had been given to Mrs. Thompson's lawyer. It was a special request for her last will and testament. The page read:

I, Ideila Thompson, would like to leave Valoria Thomas the sum of 350,000 dollars out of my savings of a million dollar. She is to be issued the funds immediately after my death by way of her signature. I am no kin of this woman. I met her in the grocery store. She did a great deed. She did what I should have done a long time ago, helped others. Because of her good works and kind heart, she deserves a part of what I have worked so hard to build. May God bless her and her family. In my last words, I would like for her to read this last will. If you are reading this letter, Ms. Valoria, I want you to know that you helped me. Thank you and keep up the good work.

Signed,
The quiet old lady with a new purse

"Charity?" Val called out.
"Yes, Val?" Charity replied.
"Please come here."

"Is everything okay? What's wrong, Val? Why are you crying?"
"Do you remember the little old lady who came in here?"
"Yes."
"She died of breast cancer."
"That is what I forgot to tell you."
"What?" Val asked, surprised.

"My grandmother knows her," said Charity. "I saw the old lady one day about three weeks ago. I was taking my grandmother to get her medicine. The old lady was walking as if she was lost. I remembered who she was, and I told my grandmother where I had seen her before and how weird she was. My grandmother told me that this woman's name was Mrs. Thompson. She told me she was filthy rich. She told me that her husband owned a railroad company, and right before he got sick, he sold it and gave his wife everything even before he died. She said the woman was very stingy and would walk over the poor. She said the first time she saw her was at the light company. She said Mrs. Thompson was driving the fanciest cars, wearing the fanciest clothes, and sporting the finest handbags so she could keep her money in the best. Something changed that day when she was in the light company. She said she was about three customers behind Mrs. Thompson and there were two customers in front of her. She said Mrs. Thompson was standing right behind her friend who was just as loaded. The woman who was in front of Mrs. Thompson's friend was a young girl who had a small child. The girl was pleading the worker to keep her lights on because it was cold and she could only pay what she could. The worker told her she needed to come up with eighty dollars and she would keep her lights on. The girl only had fifty-six dollars. She then got loud with the woman and everyone began to hear what was going on. She said she saw Mrs. Thompson look down at her purse but she did not say anything. She said the young girl left crying, holding her baby. My grandmother said the next month she ended up in the light company again at the same time as Mrs. Thompson, but this time, she was standing behind Mrs. Thompson. Just so happen, the same lady was taking payments. When Mrs. Thompson got to the line, she must have felt bad and remembered the young girl because she asked the woman what happened to the young girl. The worker grabbed her hand and sadly said, 'I feel so bad.' The girl died from the cold, and because no one knew she was dead, the baby was in the house, alive, for two days. The baby cried and kicked the covers off of it and died the same day they found them. When Mrs. Thompson left, every time someone saw her after that, she did not drive her cars and she did not wear her fancy clothes. They said she would only carry her new bags, for she had a thousand of them. She hardly ever spoke to anyone. My grandmother says she thinks she felt so bad that she did not give her the twenty-four dollars to keep her lights on. She knew that she could have made a difference in someone's life. Because of the pride of wanting to keep her purse full, she punished herself. That is so sad about her, though. My phone is ringing, hold on."

Val just sat there and stared at the form before signing. Val signed the form and dropped it in the DHL pick-up box downstairs in the lobby. As she was leaving for the evening, while she was driving, she began to cry from compassion for the old woman who passed away.

The next day, Val arrived at the office a little early to compare figures with this month's profits after bills were paid out. Val noticed that she had dropped 3,000 dollars in donations since last month. Val had been in business now for five years. The average donations for a month would range anywhere from 6,000 to 9,000 dollars. She had seen many people, including a few famous faces. Some of her gift contributions came from normal-working people who were not rich. Some lived comfortable lives and some had it hard at times, but they were so grateful for the help that she had given them that they gave unselfishly or without worry. Her donations mainly came from wealthy people who she had never met. Because she might have helped someone in their family, they appreciated it so much that they wanted to see her business stand, so many donated because they felt obligated and many were touched by the way she operated. The gift contribution she had received from the old woman was, by far, the largest she had received from one individual.

The next day, Charity arrived at the office on time. "Hey, Val," Charity greeted.

"Hey, Char!" Val responded.

"You have one appointment for today. Charlene is scheduled for 10:30 A.M. I think that you might have at least two walk-ins because I had two different women call and ask for directions yesterday."

"Okay, thanks."

Val then had a light shine in her eyes. She closed them while she was trying to gain focus. While she had her eyes closed, many thoughts began running through her head, bad and good. Instantly, she began to pray silently, Saying, "Lord, remove this confusion from my head. It is trying to distract me and bring me back down to the gutter from which you helped me escape from. Please, remove them now." She then opened her eyes quickly. At that moment, the thoughts ceased. "Thank you, Lord. Once again, you have spared me. I don't know why those thoughts came to me so suddenly. I do not receive those thoughts because I am your child, and by your grace, you have given me serenity. I have peace in my life. No thought can bring me down anymore." Val then walked over to her bookshelf where her envelopes were. There was a knock at the door before it slowly opened. It was Charlene.

"Hey, Val, how are you?" Charlene greeted.

"I am blessed. How are you this morning, Charlene?" Val responded.

"Well, Val, it seems that every time I try to think positive and I start to feel a little happy, something always comes up to bring me down," Charlene confided. Val turned and looked at her with understanding because, minutes before she walked through the door, the same thing had just happened to her. "I have started praying and trying to read my Bible more. After I pray and read, I feel good, then just as soon as I am away from it, for at least thirty minutes, I begin to have thoughts and regrets, and I start to feel bad all over again. I just feel like God has given up on me because even though I am trying, I can't get a break just for a moment."

"When do you have these thoughts the most?" Val asked.

"They usually come when I am in a relaxed mood," answered Charlene, "right as I am waking up, on my lunch break, and sometimes, when I am about to go to bed. I was taking a bubble bath last night, and while I was lying there, enjoying the candles and the soft music, I began to cry, and all of a sudden, I just started to hate who I am all over again. Val, I can't do this anymore. You have tried to help me the best way you can. You have helped me see some things I probably would have never seen if I hadn't have heard it from you, but I know that no one can help me. This is my life, and so I must deal with it by myself. I feel that I am a thorn in your side because I keep coming here and I have not been able to see all of the light that you say is there. Val, I can't do this anymore."

"Charlene, I want you to pinch yourself on the arm," said Val after listening to what Charlene had to say.

"What is that supposed to do, make me wake up from a bad dream?" asked Charlene, surprised by Val's instruction.

"Just do it for yourself, please." So, Charlene pinched herself on the arm as much as she could stand. "Did you feel that pinch, Charlene?"

"Yes, I surely did."

"So, you know that pain is real, and if you had applied more pressure to your arm, do you believe you would have felt more pain than what you just did?"

"I know I would have, without a doubt."

"How do you know it would have been worse if you have never pinched yourself that hard? Maybe the pain would have stayed the same. How do you know if you never tried to pinch yourself worse?"

"I just know for a fact that it would have. I don't have to pinch myself that hard to know that it would have hurt worse. That is just something you just know."

"Like that pinch that you just know could be worse, do you not think there is a God because you have not seen him?" asked Val. "Do you not think your situation can get better if you just trust him? What do you have to lose? How would you know, like that pinch, if you have never tried him before?"

Charlene looked at Val with a questioning expression. "I understand what you are saying. I have tried everything pertaining to my faith, but it's not working for me. I just don't know how to do that."

"It's easy, the same way you trust in that pinch that can hurt worse," responded Val.

Charlene began to cry. Her visit lasted for another twenty minutes. Charlene then left and made another appointment with Val in two weeks. Val knew that it would take Charlene a little longer than others to find her serenity, but as long as she did not give up and kept trying after each fall, she would one day remove the training wheels from her bike of life.

Three weeks had passed since she signed the will to accept her gift from the little old bag lady. Monday morning, Val came into the office a little late that day because Isaac had a dentist's appointment. When she walked into her office, she noticed a certified check on her desk. She thought that it was the 350,000 dollars from the old lady. Indeed, it was the check from the insurance company. Val then gathered her keys and told Charity to reschedule all walk-ins for the day. When she left, she went to the light company. When Val arrived, she requested to see the person in charge of the accounts. When the manager came out, he was wearing a name tag that read Timothy Watkins. "Hello, my name is Valoria Thomas. If you have a minute, I would like to speak with you in private," Val said.

"Sure," Timothy replied. They walked through two doors and down a long hallway to his office. His office space was really small. Val thought to herself, *Thank you, Lord, for the office you gave me.* Val's personal office could fit four of his. "What can I do for you, Miss Valoria?" Timothy asked.

"Well, I would like to pay everyone's residential light bill in your city database that is past due or has doubled because of nonpayment on their last bill," Val answered.

"Are you sure you want to do that?" asked Timothy, startled and skeptical about Val's statement. "That can cost you more than what you are expecting."

"Well, we will see," said Val. "Depending on the cost of the city alone, if there are funds left, then we can handle some outskirt light bills."

"How will you be handling these charges?"

"Certified funds."

"Okay, I would first like to get some information from you."

"I would rather not be broadcasted or presented any award from you or your company," Val said to the manager. "So the only thing you will need from me is my name, if you need that. I want to be strictly confidential."

"Okay, but before we accept your monies, we just need to verify that you are the person whom the check is for and that the funds were awarded to you from the insurance company legally."

"That's fine. Do what you need. I will just wait." The man then left the room in disbelief of what was about to happen. He then came in and out of the office to check on Val over the course of two hours. He then returned with a woman who was an administrator of operations. She introduced herself and let Val know that everything checked out with the verifications, and that she thought that what Val was doing was a great thing.

"While we were verifying your information, we came up with a total for our past due residential records. The total is 289,000.78 dollars, that's for the city. The outskirt cities that have lights with us total to 18,500 dollars in past due."

"Let's start," Val suggested.

"All we need for you to do is sign this form so we can start the process. We will issue you a certified check for the remaining balance." They then preceded the process and informed Val that it would be tomorrow. When they could get a list of the paid account numbers with the amount to show proof of payments, Val then took her receipt and her change of 42,499.22 dollars and went to her bank to deposit it in her business account.

When she got back to the office, there was another certified check. It was a donation to the company from the actress, Sharron. The note read: *"I don't know what it is about you, but I will tip you anyway."* There was a check for 1,000 dollars.

That week had started out great. A few days had passed; it was now Thursday. Val came into the office. "You have two appointments for today, Allen and Leia," Charity said.

"Okay, just buzz me when they arrive," Val answered.

In the garage, Allen and Leia arrived at the same time, even though their appointments were an hour and a half apart. Leia was a little early, hoping that the appointment before her would not show. It had been about six months since Allen had seen Leia at the stoplight. When Allen got out of his car, he did not recognize her. Leia knew who he was, though. As they were going up the elevator, Allen said, "Have I seen you somewhere before?"

"Yes, you first saw me here. I looked a little different the first time you seen me. I was also at the stoplight one day next to your car," Leia replied.

Allen looked at her in amazement. He did not know what to say because she made a drastic change since he had last seen her. She actually was beautiful. She started eating healthy and working out every day to eliminate the stress she felt. She went and got contacts instead of wearing her glasses. She started going shopping for the love of herself. Even though she had big feet, she decided to buy shoes that would not bring attention to her feet, shoes that were not dark and solid. She did not put on a lot of makeup, but she started using natural herbs to cleanse her skin.

"Good morning!" Charity greeted.

"Good morning!" Allen and Leia said in unison.

"Val will be with you in a moment." Charity called out to her boss, "Val?"

"Yes, Charity?" Val replied.

"Both appointments are here. Allen's appointment is first."

"Okay, thanks, send Allen in first."

The day was about over when Val's phone rang. "This is Valoria," Val said.

"Hello, Ms. Thomas, this is Karen Krutch, I am the president of the electric company. I am calling to extend my gratitude for what you did for our past due customers. Because of you, we were able to meet our quota this month, for the first time in five years, in past due accounts. I also would like to tell you that every customer you helped wants to know your name and who you are, but because of confidentiality, we cannot disclose that information to them. Now, we are starting to receive cards and thank you letters on your behalf—"

Before she could finish, Valoria interrupted, saying, "I'm sorry, Ms. Karen. I don't mean to cut you off, but I refuse to take the credit for any good deed that I have carried out. I'm just thankful that God chose me to be in place when he blessed those families. I don't mean to run, but I have to go and pick up my son. I am just like those families—I have a life. The only thing I can tell you is that when they call and want to know so badly, just tell them God did it and he is the one they should thank. If you don't mind, I would appreciate no more phone calls. Thank you for your gratitude, but I only did what my heart led me to do. And for that, it was my reward to be the one who God used. Thank you! Goodbye."

When Val hung up the phone, she felt so good that she had given God what so many refused to do, and that was give him all the glory and take none for herself because without God, she would have put that money in the bank and took off work for two months. But because she allowed the Lord to work, she was not concerned with the riches of this world. She had one nice car that God gave her and a nice house that God gave her, and last but not the least, she worked for herself, and because she was faithful, God paid her.

Before she left the office for the day,

Valoria tried to wait around for as long as she could, hoping that Charity would ask to leave early because she did not have any more appointments for the day and she wanted to put a surprise on her desk. So, she decided to go ahead, leave, and come back after she picked up her son.

The next morning, Val arrived a little early because she wasn't able to make it back last night. When she got there, she wrote a check to Charity for 10,000 dollars, a bonus check. Even though she paid her well already, Val felt that everyone could use a lot of extra sometimes. She decided to put it where she would find it if she was frustrated and looking for something, under her calendar on her desk. Valoria knew that every time Charity got frustrated, she looked under the calendar, like whatever it was she was looking for would mysteriously appear under the calendar. Val did that because she knew she would find it when she needed it most. She had learned that Charity hid her emotions really well, and when she was stressed, she moved around a lot, but never did she tell Val what's going on.

Charity arrived at work on time and began preparing for the day. Val never expected for Charity to get frustrated this early. Charity kept a green folder with new client info, so that she could update her computer when she had downtime later on that morning. Charity had forgotten that she had taken it home by mistake, so she became a little frustrated and began looking in and under everything. The first place she looked was under her calendar. She noticed there was a blank envelope that was sealed. She opened it up. "Vaaaaallllllllllll! Is this a joke?" Charity was startled.

"What?" Val replied, pretending to know nothing.

"This check written to me from you for 10,000 dollars," she exclaimed, thrusting the check at Val as though her boss hadn't seen it before.

"No, Ma'am, it is totally real," replied Valoria, smiling.

"Val, why are you giving me this? What are you doing?"

"Why do I have to be doing anything? Why don't you ask God why? It was laid on my heart to do this for you, and so, I followed my heart."

Charity began to cry hysterically. She cried so hard that she fell to her knees in front of Val's desk. Val had to assist Charity to the chair, so that she could get herself together.

Allen and Leia arrived at the same time once again, but this time, Allen was early. They sat in the lobby, waiting for Val to finish up with a new client she had. While they were sitting and waiting, they began laughing about meeting up at the same time again. Leia, at this point, had really changed from the person she used to be. Allen had begun to accept his situation. He was still torn emotionally, but he was steadily moving on.

"So, Leia, I wonder how many times we are going to show up at the same time," Allen said.

"Ha-ha! I was wondering the same thing. So, Allen, if you don't mind me asking, what type of work do you do?" Leia replied.

"Well, I am a mortgage broker. I started off in real estate."

"That's interesting. I was going to look into getting in that business. I just have had so much going on. I have not had time to look into it."

"Perhaps, I can gather some information for you, so that you could look more into it. I can leave the info with Val to give to you."

"That will be great. Just in case I have any questions about any of the material, do you mind me asking for your number? I will also give you my contact info so you can let me know when you get it."

"Sure, that should not be a problem," replied Allen. "You are considering a good business to be in."

At this point, Val was done with her appointment. "Well, hello, Leia and Allen, give me about three minutes and I will be ready for whoever is next," Val greeted.

Allen gave Leia his info. She then stood up to proceed to walk into the office. Before she walked into the door, she looked back out of the corner of her eye to see if Allen was watching her. He, unfortunately, was looking down with his hands folded together. She stood there for about thirty seconds, wondering if he was flirting or just making conversation. She walked on in the office, thinking that, at this point, he was in no way interested in her. She felt as if it was and always would be business to the men she met. Leia knew that she was a very business-minded person and that the men who she had met in the past admired her drive for success, so they would befriend her for the encouragement to become a go-getter like herself.

"I must say, Leia, you have really blossomed from when we first started our sessions," Val said.

"Val, can I ask you a question without getting in your business too much?" Leia asked.

"Sure."

"Why are you single? And how do you know, when you meet a man, he is the one for you?"

"Well, the answer to your first question is: I am single by choice," replied Val. "I am waiting on God to send me a king. I am going to trust God for everything, first and always, and if the Lord wants to bless me with a man, he will do so. I have had many opportunities to have a man, but I refuse to trust my own fleshly judgment because it has always failed me. When I was wild and not trying to live right, I chose nothing but messes that I didn't know was a mess until everything went wrong and I was hurt in the result of it. The answer to your second question is: you will only know if he is the one if God tells you that he is. He may not speak to you directly, but you will feel it in your heart that his pursuing you is not that of a common man, a typical woman chaser. God, for one, would have led him to you, and he will be seeking for a wife according to his instructions."

"I somewhat understand what you are saying," Leia said. "I just don't see how we could understand when God would speak to us. How would we know it is God speaking and not our own intuition?"

"If you feel that your decision came from your own thoughts, then you know it is not God, but if your decision came from your heart and it is a wise and pure choice that is good, then you know that it's probably our father," Val said. "Normally, people do not know the difference between the feeling that comes from the heart and the feeling that comes from the mind. Your flesh has its own feelings that you recognize from the beginning because they normally are bad for the soul. The best advice I can give you concerning discerning what you hear is to continue to pray that the Lord gives you understanding. If you stay true to your prayer, God will hear you, and on his time, he will give you what you ask for. Just stay focused and continue to seek him and the understanding, and you will see things that you never knew were there."

Later that evening, Val was finishing up for the day when she heard a small voice whispering around her, saying, "To God be the glory. His praise shall continually be in my mouth." Val began to cry and worship in her office while thanking God for every sign, every dream, and every good choice she made. She thanked him continuously for keeping her when she was out in the world doing wrong. He kept her because he knew she would be faithful once her change had been made. Because she was determined to stay faithful, he blessed her in ways she never expected.

A couple of weeks had passed, and another Monday arrived once again. "Good morning Val, your first appointment is in thirty minutes. It's Zack," Charity said.

"Wow!" Val said.

"You don't have to worry about him flirting. He has a girlfriend now."

"Really? And how do you know?" asked Val.

"Well, I was out in a restaurant with my cousin, Tracy, and we saw him walking to his car. He recognized me and came over to speak. I don't know what happened after that. All I know is that he has been going out with my cousin, Tracy, ever since," replied Charity.

"Wow!" was all Val could muster. Val then walked in her office. She noticed her message light was blinking, which was kind of odd because the calls usually stop at Charity's desk, unless they have her personal line. Val sat down at her desk, about to check her message, but before she picked up the receiver, she felt chills roll down her spine. She was unnerved because she did not know why she got that feeling. It was like maybe she had to brace herself before she picked up that phone. Val then went to get a cup of coffee. When she returned to her office to check her message, Zack had arrived. She decided to take the appointment before she checked the message.

"Hello, Ms. Val," Zack greeted.

"How are you doing, Zack?" Val responded.

"I am never better. I still have been under a sex spell, but I have accepted that this spell will never be broken. All I need is a woman to control me now."

"Zack, I know someone who can be whatever you want them to be if you trust them and know that the spell can be broken and controlled to the point you forget you were ever like that."

"Where is this someone at?" asked Zack.

"Right here in this room!" Zack began to look around as though he was anxious to meet this person. "That's right. Everywhere you look, Jesus is there."

"Oh, you're talking about Jesus. I thought you were talking about a real person."

"God is more real than we will ever be, Zack."

"I have tried to believe in God, but it is so hard because everything I have ever prayed for never came to me," retorted Zack. "So that is my story of praying and waiting for God to help me."

"I feel so sad that you would say such a thing like that," said Val. "Zack, you are very successful. You have more than most people have—a good job, nice car, money in the bank, and you are very handsome. God has blessed you and all that you are about. It's because of him that you are breathing, eating, sleeping, speaking, and every simple thing that you are able to do. You cannot believe that you conceived and created yourself. You have what you have because he allowed you to get these things. Whatever pain that you endured in your past has contributed to the man that you are today. You cannot blame your past on no one, even if it was not your fault. So many of us need to take that bad and painful past and make it into a strong footstool, to stand proud and tall. Because of God's mercy, we were able to withstand and survive through the times that came to destroy us." At this point, Val had gotten Zack's attention, but this time, he could not believe what was coming out of her mouth. He had never sat in her session long enough to hear the wise words of a servant of God.

"You are serious about your work, huh?" said Zack.

"As long as I continue to live, I will always be serious."

Zack then stood and proceeded to walk out of the office as if he had been insulted, but he appreciated it. "Goodbye, Val."

"Goodbye, Zack." God had, at that very moment, moved that temptation out of her way.

When Zack left, Val had no idea that she would never hear from him ever again. Val had sat down and breathed deep because the whole time Zack was in her office, she thought he was the reason she had chills, but for some reason, the chills were still there. Val finally picked up the phone to check her message. She was surprised to hear the voice of her ex-husband's girlfriend. "Val, this is Shonte. I really need to talk to you, so if you could, please give me a call as soon as possible." Val was very stunned at this point because she did not know what to expect to hear from this woman. Val then took about five minutes to regroup and called her.

"Hello!" Shonte, or Shay as she was more commonly known, greeted.

"Hello, Shay, this is Val. I just got around to call you. What's going on?" Val asked.

"You wouldn't by any chance have heard from Johnathan" asked Shay by way of answer.

Again, this puzzled Val even the more because Shay lived with him for four years, and she should know by now that Val does not want him. "No, I haven't. Is everything all right?"

"No, Val, he has not been home in three days. He has not called, and his phone is off," replied Shay. "I just don't know what to think. I thought we were happy, and then again, you know he is still in those streets."

"Oh, my, have you reported him missing?"

"Yes, I called this morning and made a missing person report."

"Where did you last see him?"

"Well, we had just made love, and he left to go and meet someone, but never came back. It's like his street life is so personal that he does not tell me anything. I don't even know the name of the person he was going to meet."

Now, at this point, Val was really uncomfortable asking questions because Shay was very open and blunt. Besides, who wanted to know what their ex was doing with someone else? "Well, maybe he will show up at some point. If I hear from him, I will be sure to tell him how selfish he is for not telling someone he is okay." When they hung up the phone, Val felt a little disturbed by the information. Val knew that she would have to tell her son because today was the day he was supposed to come and get Isaac to buy him a game.

When Val got home, she cooked Isaac his favorite meal and made him his favorite dessert: Hamburger Helper with extra cheese and chocolate cupcakes with chocolate icing. Isaac was very excited.

"Isaac, come here for a minute, baby," Val said.

"Yes, Ma'am," Isaac replied.

"Sit down for a minute. I want to talk to you." Isaac sat down next to Val on her bed and laid his head on her shoulder. "Baby, there is something

Serenity They Seek

Mommy has to tell you, but before I do, I want you to know I stopped and picked up that game you wanted."

"Mom, you know my daddy was going to take me to get it. Now, he probably won't have a reason to come by."

"Baby, daddy will be unable to take you to get a game because he is missing," said Val.

Isaac sat straight up and said, "Missing? What's that mean, Mom? He's lost?"

"Yes, baby, he is lost, and no one knows where he is right now," answered Val gently.

"Mom, why would he get himself lost?" Isaac asked. "And he knows he promised he was going to take me to get a new game."

"Baby, we don't know if he did it on purpose."

"Is he dead, Mommy?"

"I hope not, baby." Isaac began to cry and held Val really tight, so she said, "Let me tell you something, Isaac. Do you remember what Mommy told you to do when you feel frustrated?"

"Yes, Ma'am, you said pray and ask God to help me," replied Isaac.

"I want you to always remember that, no matter what. Isaac, no matter what happens to Daddy or Mommy, you have to continue to live your life. Don't ever feel you have nothing or no one if your parents are gone. Always remember that Jesus is your mother and father always."

"But, Mom, what if nanny dies and I have to go to one of those homes until I get older?"

"Baby, I have already prayed over you and claimed your soul for Jesus, so if you have to go to a home and you stray from what I teach you, remember: never forget God. Never stop believing in Jesus. Always keep him in your heart, and one day, he will rescue you and use you for his purpose."

"He will, Mom? Will I be like you, but as a boy?"

"Yes, baby, but you will be better than me, as a man." After talking to Isaac, Val sung him to sleep while holding him to make him feel secure. Val then got on her knees and began to pray for her ex who had now become a missing person.

The next morning, when Val arrived at work, she decided to call Shay to ask if she had heard from him. "Hello, Shay, have you heard from him yet?" Val said.

Shay said in a very faint and depressed voice, "No, we sure haven't." After staying on the phone for about ten minutes with Shay, Val hung up the phone, and instantly, she became sad, hoping that he was all right. Val could not help but be concerned.

It was Friday morning and her ex-husband was still missing. Val had been praying every day since that day. She even cried a few times because she was in disbelief that someone this close to her would actually become missing in this big world.

"Val, your 12-noon appointment is here," Charity said.

"Send them in," Val instructed. Val had gone into a silent prayer, asking the Lord to give her strength, before the door opened. She knew that she had to maintain her composure, for so many people depended on her dedication to her work. When Val looked up, in walked Keasha, the young girl who came to see her about six months ago. Val was surprised at what she was seeing. Keasha looked to be as if she was five months pregnant. Keasha sat down on the chair and began to cry.

"I know I messed up really bad, Ms. Val. I should have listened to you when I left here. Instead, I was stupid. Please don't look down on me," Keasha said.

"Oh, no, sweetie, I would never look down on you," Val assured her gently. "We all have made choices we feel we would later regret. That does not mean that God looks at us any different." Val walked over to the chair and hugged Keasha to reassure her that everything would be fine.

"I came to see you, Ms. Val, because I didn't know what else to do or anyone else to talk to."

"Do you have somewhere to stay?"

"Yes, Ma'am, I'm staying at home with my mother. Everything has been cool so far, but I can tell that later, we are going to have problems. My child's father has moved in with another girl, and I'm stuck pregnant, living with my mother. I feel so ashamed. What is wrong with me, Ms. Val? I am so stupid."

"Keasha, the first advice I am going to give you is to stop downing yourself. If God is allowing you to carry another human being, you need to feel privileged," said Val. "I'm not saying be happy about what you did, but I am saying don't be too unhappy, either. Children are special gifts from God. Yes, some of us do have children early; some wait until they are old. But whatever the case is, I feel that 90 percent of childbirths make some of us more responsible and grateful for life itself. Yes, you may have made a bad choice and got pregnant in the process, but always remember that your choices could be your destiny, and on the other hand, your choices can be your destroyer. That all depends on how well you bounce back from the course of your choice."

"What about if you've already seen the bad that is about to happen from that point of your decision and so on?" Keasha asked.

"In seeing the bad, have you seen it as good in any way?"

"No, I guess I have not. The only thing I see is me as a single parent, struggling while living with my mom."

"Keasha, I want you to do something for me."

"What's that?" she asked.

"When you leave my office today, I want you to get a notebook and a pencil, and you only will write within this notebook," Val said. "I want you to go home and fix yourself whatever it is you like to drink." Val went to her cabinet that sat in the corner of her office and pulled out a case of CDs. "Do you have a CD player?"

"A small one."

"Good, take this CD, put it in, and listen to it. After you get comfortable, I want you to open up your notebook and write down everything good that can come out of your situation. Now, in order for you to understand why I am having you to do this, you have to write in it every day or as much as you can."

"I need to know, Ms. Valoria, what is that supposed to do?"

"If I tell you, it will defeat the purpose," replied Val. "Just do it, and later, you will see for yourself why I advised you do it. I can give you a million reasons why I think you should, but they will all just be my reasons. I want you to put your use for it, whatever you can, and define your own reasons. While you are writing, just write. Don't try to figure it out like a puzzle because you will never understand that way. By you being so young, there is so much knowledge you have yet to come into."

"That still does not change the fact that I might get worse when the baby gets here. Who's to say?"

"Like I said, I can go on for days with you because there is so much information you desire, but the time is when God say you are ready," said Val. "I also want you to pick up your Bible, open it up, and whatever chapter it lands on, pick a verse or paragraph and read after every writing. I want you to come back and see me in one month. I never give repeat session requests, but for you, I want to update your results periodically. I think if you stay extremely positive right now, you will be able to deal with your situation a whole lot better, which will cause your results to be a whole lot more tolerable."

"Update my results? What makes me so different?"

"You are my youngest client, Keasha. That makes me very concerned and careful about the advice I give." After she sat and explained why she was concerned, Keasha left the office and stopped by Charity's desk to schedule a requested routine follow-up meeting.

That day, Val was feeling a little overwhelmed due to the fact that they still had not found Isaac's father. So, she decided to continue working outside the office. She went to the local mental institution to visit some of the residents and pray for them. As she visited some of the wards that she was allowed to visit, she noticed as she was leaving that they were bringing someone in, strapped down and fighting the entire time. She moved to the side so that they may pass. Val began to pray instantly for the calming of this young lady. While passing, the woman looked up at Val and stared as if she recognized a familiar face. "Wait!" Val yelled at the orderly. They stopped and turned to see why she stopped them. Val walked up to the lady and called her by her name. "Alonda?" Val said. Val recognized her because she was one of her clients, about two years ago. When she stopped seeing Val, she heard from other sources that Alonda had changed for the better.

"Ma'am, I'm sorry, but we must move on," the orderly said.

"I'm sorry. I use to be her counselor. I thought she would recognize me," Val responded.

Alonda was staring at Val, but was not saying a word. As they began to walk away, Alonda turned around and screamed, "Val, I gave up on him. Please pray for me." Val turned around instantly and watched as they rolled her through the door. Alonda, at this point, had turned all the way around and looked at Val with large tears in her eyes. Before the door closed behind her, she said it again very faintly, "I just gave up!" When Val got to the front desk to sign out, she started to cry because she remembered their sessions clearly at that point. It saddened her to know that she was being admitted to a mental ward, and she truly was not crazy. Alonda started to see Val right after her divorce from her husband of thirteen years. They never had any kids, but her husband cheated and had a baby with another woman. She forgave him and stayed with him, but a few years later, she found out he had two more kids, one before her time, and another during their marriage. Alonda became so depressed. She left him because she could no longer deal with his selfish ways. Alonda was also molested as a child. She was hurt and upset, but after seeing Val for eight months, she gained self-confidence to search for her own happiness.

When Val got home, she prayed and began to work on her material for the class she was going to teach at the convention. While she was working, Isaac came in her office with a bouquet of flowers he plucked out of her garden. He tied them together with a Band-Aid. Valoria was very touched. She cried and hugged him. Even though she had a bad day, she continued to press her way. Her son brightened the day that had been dim.

The day had begun at the office when Charity called in Val's office. "Val, are you taking walk-ins today?"

"How many appointments do I have today?" Val asked.

"Six," Charity replied.

"That's fine. Who is it?"

"It's Allen."

"Okay, that's fine. Send him in." When Allen walked in, he was very calm but with a very disappointed look on his face. "Allen, why the sad face?" Val asked.

"Because Antwan is not here to see his son," Allen said.

Val stood up as if she had seen a ghost. "His son?"

"Yes, Val, he was born in the downtown Memorial Hospital. His mother only spent one hour with him before they took her back to prison. The child is in foster care now. They allowed her to make three phone calls to family members to see if anyone could take the baby so that he would not be in state custody. When she called me, I could not even say anything. I went to the foster home to see him." All of a sudden, Allen began to cry as he sat down on the chair.

"I understand why this would be hard for you, Allen."

"Val, I've seen him. He looks like Antwan when he was a baby. I know that I do not need a paternity test. He looks like my son when he was born."

"Have you decided on what you are going to do?"

"Yes, Val, I've got to get him out of state custody. Antwan would want me to do that. I just don't know if I could be a single parent at the age that I am now."

"Well, you know, Allen, as long as you trust God from which commeth your help, he will provide you with assistance. God sees and knows all of your worries and concerns. As long as you trust in him, he will always make a way."

"You are right, Val. I have made it this far because of God," agreed Allen. "I am so glad that he put you in my path as my counselor. I am grateful to be able to have someone to talk to besides my walls."

"Allen, if you don't mind, can I ask you a question?"

"Anything, Val."

"Do you ever want to be married?" Val asked.

"Well, Val, that is a good question. I don' think I have put much thought into settling down, but it would be nice to have a special someone to help me in my journey in starting over as a father," Allen answered.

"Well, you know, if that is something you really are thinking about, I think it would be good for you. I feel that you are never too old to have a family and be happy. There are some people who do not find happiness until they get old. What might seem late to some people, is right on time for others."

"You see, Val, that is going to be my only problem, finding that special someone."

"Yes, Allen, that will be a problem for you, but not for God. That is the problem of so many people. We feel that we can find our own mates based on our own standards and wants. It is always the best for a man to seek, but in doing so, you must consult God first. Tell him what you are looking for, and he will give you the true desire of your heart."

"But that does not make sense to me. Why would I tell him one thing, but mean another?"

"Because, naturally, that is the way our bodies work," said Val. "Your mind can draw you a totally different picture than what your heart has drawn. You see, your mind actually puts it into motion by your thoughts of seeing it. But your heart puts it in the order it needs to be. You never know what to expect when it comes from the heart because your heart never wants to hurt."

"That is so true, Val. I never thought about it that way. Maybe that's why so many of my relationships have failed in the past because I was so caught up in the way a woman looked and what I wanted. I possibly looked over what God had planned for what I needed."

"Like I said before, Allen, things are not laid out in a schedule format for our lives. We have to thank God for every morning we see and every breath we take. It very well may not have been your time then, but it may now be the time. We all develop a past, whether good or bad. I feel that we should let our past help us heal. I'm not saying rethink over what has come and gone, but I am saying if you made it through that triumph, you should realize that you are a little stronger today than yesterday."

"I understand, Val," Allen said. "Thank you for all of the wise advices you give me. I don't know where my mind would be if it was not for you."

"Do not thank me, thank God, because I don't know where my mind would be if it was not for him."

They both agreed, and Allen left with a smile.

Val went home and realized that she only had four days to prepare for her seminar. So she instantly got into her Bible and began to seek out Scriptures that would back up her teaching to the women who would attend. As she was seeking in her Bible, she ran across a Scripture that she had noticed before, but her understanding was somewhat different then. She began to pray for a better interpretation of its meaning. For some reason, Val knew that this could be a good reason why she ran up on this Scripture—it was in the same lines of the seminar she was going to conduct. It was 1 Timothy 2:9-10. As she began to read through her Bible, something happened; she began to get sad. Val knew what it was because it was something that would come to her every blue moon, when she was deep in thought. Val closed her Bible and began to pray that the feeling that she was having would go away. Val prayed for one hour and forty-five minutes before that feeling faded. When she was done, she wiped her tears and continued her studies.

The next day, when Val went to work, she was a little tired from staying up late preparing for her seminar. When she arrived, her first client was already there. "Hello, Leia, come on back. How are you today?" Val greeted. Who knew that this woman who Val had met almost a year ago would transform into the beautiful, confident woman she had become? Leia, once with low self-esteem and overweight, with no personal goals, was very different at this point.

"Hello, Val, I'm doing great. I am so happy with myself now," Leia responded. Leia began to cry and said, "I don't know what I would have done without you. You have been such a life saver."

"No, Leia, I haven't. God has," Val replied. "You see, Leia, the one thing that I know is when you are down and feel there is no hope anywhere, God will sometimes put people in your life to help you get going in the right direction. But, it's up to you to accept or reject help. I can only advise you to try another path, and the rest is up to you. You have some people who will take all of the credit for helping a person change his or her situation, and then you have some people who will let you find your own joy in your success. When it is all said and done, it's still in God's will that you were able or about to find the peace you seek with your whole heart. Leia, I am so proud of you, and I am glad to say that you must continue your journey without me. Of course, I will always be here if you need me, but look up to God first and always ask for direction and help. It's because of him that I was able to be there for you."

Leia began to smile and gave Val a hug. "Val, I will keep you updated on my life. Please continue to pray for me, Val, that I will continue on the happy path I am on for the first time in my life. I still don't have a husband, but it's okay because I love myself now, which is more important than anything. I have never liked or even loved who I am, but I can honestly say that I love myself with all of my flaws."

When Leia left, she was glowing and just about skipping. She was holding her head so high. Val watched her as she walked out of the office. Then, Val went back to her desk and pulled out her computer files and noted in the file for Leia Serenity. It had been a little while since she was able to write that in anyone's file, but she did it with excitement because she knew in her heart that Leia would always remember that God used Val to help her, and for that, she would be grateful and, hopefully, build an awesome relationship with God, always thanking him for saving her mind, body, and soul.

Val had two new clients whose appointments went pretty quickly. When she was done with her last client for the day, she walked out to Charity's desk to check appointments for the next day, then she noticed Tamya getting off the elevator. She did not have an appointment, and the day was just about over. Val did not know what to expect from this surprise visit.

"Val, please, tell me you have a minute," Tamya said.

"Sure, come on in," Val responded. While she was walking to her office, Val noticed Tamya had a smile on her face.

"Val, I know my visit is unexpected," Tamya said. "I tried to get here earlier, but I did not have anyone to watch my kids. My cell phone is cut off, so I could not call to let you know I needed to see you today. I needed to tell you what I have done for the last two weeks. I know, when I came in here last month, I was high on weed and cocaine. I still want to apologize for that, Val. I know you knew I was loaded, but you still talked to me like I was not. I even heard you when you walked toward your desk and asked the Lord to come in and speak for you. For some reason, I was still able to hear everything you were saying. I even remembered some of it. The one thing that touched me the most, Val, was when I was leaving you, you told me softly, 'Tamya, don't give up.' Val, I want you to know for these past two weeks, I finally feel the fight that I have deep down, and I am finally allowing myself to fight back. I realize a lot of things that I did not before. I feel lonely for companionship sometimes. I realized that every time I get that feeling, I feel like I have to do some kind of drug to try to get my mind off that feeling. Instead, I realize that it only enhances it, and it makes me desperate to fill that void at the time. I have had the opportunity to smoke and even do pills, but what you said has been standing out in my mind. Val, I don't want to give up my life to these streets. I realize I do love my kids, and as long as the Lord allows me to have breath in my body, I should cherish every moment I spend with them. Val, I finally understand. I didn't before because my mind has been cloudy. Val, please say something."

"Ha-ha, I was just listening to you."

"Val, something else happened to me that I want to share with you."

"What happened?"

"I had a dream," replied Tamya. "It was weird, but it was a good dream, I think. I was walking on this road that was really rocky. I was walking really slow, stumbling, like my feet were hurting. I looked down at my feet and noticed that I did not have on any shoes, and around my feet were chains that connected to a long iron rod that attached to the chain that was around my waist and around my throat. I could hear the chains bumping over the rocks.

Even though I could not feel it physically, I did feel like I was feeling the pressure of the weight of it. As I continued to walk, I looked around and noticed that it was grey looking outside. I did not see any trees or buildings or anything. I just continued to walk straight. I eventually looked straight ahead and noticed that it got lighter up ahead, and far from a distance, I saw this mountain that stretched as wide as I can see. It looked as if I did not have any other way but to go up and over it. When I got closer to the mountain, the road began to get a little bit smoother—so smooth; the sound of the chains began to sound a little bit plainer. When I got to the mountain, it's like I instinctively knew to climb up, so as I began to climb, the chains became lighter, like they were melting and about to fall off at some point. I looked up but could not see a peak at all. There were no clouds or anything, just a straight mountain that had no end. I began to smile, and the sky began to lighten up. When I woke up, I felt so much better. I feel like God still loves me and that maybe my life will turn around." Tamya began to cry tears of joy softly. "Even if that dream did not mean anything specific, it gave me hope, Val. It gave me hope that, maybe, I should not give up no matter how rocky this road is and how heavy these chains are. If I keep walking, I will reach a mountain that will go nowhere but up."

Val began to smile because she knew at that point that Tamya was on the path to serenity. Val gave Tamya a hug and walked her out of the office. Val went back into her office and wrote on a notepad about Tamya's journey and put it in the top drawer of her desk.

Val and Isaac had just arrived at the hotel where the convention was going to be held. Val went to check in her room and noticed that the hotel had a fancy restaurant that converted to a full breakfast restaurant in the mornings, up until 10 A.M.

"Momma, I'm kind of hungry. Could we get something to eat after we put our things in the room?" Isaac said.

"Sure, sweetie, what do you want to eat?" Val responded.

"I want pizza."

"Okay, we will go out and find a pizza place and get you some pizza."

They both laughed as they were walking toward the elevator. As they were approaching the elevator, there were two other people standing by waiting for the doors to open. When they opened, Val and Isaac were gathering their luggage to get on, so she was not paying attention to who was exiting.

Calvin and his two friends and two women from their church were getting off. Calvin noticed Val as she was getting on after he had walked out from behind his friend. Calvin said to his friend, "She is beautiful." One of the men who was waiting to get on the elevator had offered to carry one of her suitcases. It matched the arm luggage she had on her arm, so it looked as if she was with the man. After Isaac and Val got to the room and put down their luggage, they headed back down to the lobby to get directions to the nearest pizza place. When Val asked the two women at the front desk where the nearest pizza place was, one of the receptionists told her it was about fifteen miles from the hotel. Because it was a new hotel, and they were in a secluded area, they did not have a pizza place in the area just yet.

"Because we are new and do not have a pizza place just yet, they gave us half-off coupons for the inconvenience of the guests," the front desk agent said.

"That's okay, Mom. We don't have to eat pizza. I'm hungry now. We can go in there," Isaac said, pointing at the restaurant in the hotel.

"Are you sure, sweetie?"

"Yes, Mom."

Val kissed him on the forehead and said, "I am the luckiest Mom in the world to have you as my son." Val and Isaac laughed and went into the restaurant to wait to be seated. When they were going to be seated, they could not see who was sitting behind them because the booths were so high, for privacy purposes the hotel accommodated for their guests. They knew that there would be very important people staying in their hotel who would be there for business purposes, and if they wanted to discuss their business while they ate, they should have as much privacy as possible. After they were seated, they ordered their meal, sat, and talked. After Val told Isaac how proud of him, she was, she stated, "You know Momma loves her baby."

At this time, Calvin was in the middle of his conversation with his party when he heard that voice, which spoke those very words he heard in his dream almost a year ago. His friends at his table looked at him in a strange way, as to why he lost his words. He began to finish where he left off. Even though he was talking, he was not into his own conversation. He was anxious to see the face behind the voice that he heard in his dream. It sounded like it was coming from directly behind him, but he could not turn to see. He looked around the restaurant to see in what direction the bathroom was, so he would not look so obvious. He noticed that it was in the opposite direction of where the voice was coming from. He had thought about waiting until they were done eating, but he had no idea how long the woman behind the voice had been there and if she would leave before him. He knew she had to be seated after him, but because he was with a party of five, and in deep conversation, there probably would be a lot of people who would come after and leave before them. The only way Calvin would be able to see her was if he went out of the restaurant. He had gotten so anxious to see her that he decided to leave his friends. He left his money with one of his friends and told them he would see them later at the first service of the convention. Calvin got up from the booth and turned to walk out so he could try to get a glance at the woman with the voice from his dream. Unexpectedly, the waitress was serving them at this time. When he walked by, he tried hard to look, but the waitress was in the way. He was able to get a good look at Isaac. When he walked by, Isaac looked up at him. Calvin remembered the little boy from the elevator, but he did not know exactly who he was with because there were four other women and the one man who carried the beautiful woman's luggage. When Calvin got to his room, he lay across his bed and hoped that he would see this little boy again because he would see his mother, the woman with the voice in his dream. Calvin dozed off to sleep, and because he fell asleep with that on his mind, he heard the voice again. It sounded just as clear as it did this afternoon in the restaurant. Calvin woke up out of his sleep, got on his knees, and began to pray, "Lord, if this is my wife, let me see her face. Lord, you said a man that findeth a wife findeth a good thing. I have prayed, Lord, and asked you to lead me in the right direction to find a woman of God; a faithful woman, a beautiful woman not only on the outside but also so beautiful on the inside that she is totally irresistible to my eyes."

Val and Isaac had come back from the first service of the convention. Isaac was so tired that he fell asleep in his suit. Val had to undress and put his pajamas on like she used to do when he was a toddler. When she was done, she sat, looked at her son, and said, "Lord, please make him a strong man, a loyal man, a man who will praise and serve you all the days of his life. When you bless him with a wife, Lord, give him the heart to love her unconditionally and be a great father to their kids."

The next morning, when they woke up, Isaac went to the children's workshop with a church member and her son who went to the church Val attended. Val was scheduled to do her seminar at 12 noon that Saturday. The seminar was for all women. Val had prepared very well. She was able to answer every question that was asked to her. There were a few women who did not agree with some of the things she was speaking about, but Val knew that everyone was not going to like or agree with what she was teaching. Valoria had made up in her mind that she was not going to teach on anything that was good to the ear, but what was true and by what was in accordance with the word of God. The class was scheduled for one hour and thirty minutes, but it lasted three hours and ten minutes due to deliberations. As Val got deeper into the word, she began to cry out in her heart for some direction and guidance from the Lord, so that she wouldn't be stormed mentally. Teaching and counseling may seem like an easy task, but it's actually very draining mentally. It takes a lot of study, concentration, and prayer to stay focused on developing your understanding unto others. The more Val prayed, the stronger she felt. The woman who asked her to speak was amazed at Val's research and the delivery of her message.

There had never been a women's class that lasted more than one hour and forty-five minutes. She told Val that the class was so interesting that she had everyone's attention. Val ended her message with this: "As a woman, we have many titles that are very important in this life that we live. Our responsibilities are way too important to discard even just one. Everything that we represent needs to and must follow the very instruction God gives us as the world nurturers. Even though we do not carry the seed that is life, we nurture and complete its transition. Our duties as a woman are always more extensive than a man. Always know that you are needed and appreciated by God, even when the world treats you and tell you that you are not. You are a woman, the soil of the earth."

When Val was done, she went back to her room to wait for Isaac. While she was waiting, she began to write in her journal. Shortly after, Isaac arrived and said, "Hey, Mom, how was your class?"

"It was good, baby. It was very interesting," Val responded.

"Mom, are we going to go to the gift shop so I can get Granny something?"

"Yes, Isaac, we will stop by tomorrow on our way out. Right now, we have to get rested for service tonight."

"Okay, Ma, but can I sit by Chris and his mom in the balcony?"

"That's fine, as long as I know exactly where you are." When they arrived in the convention hall at the hotel, Chris and his mom, Carolyn, were about to walk up the stairs when Chris said he needed to go to the restroom. Chris was two years older than Isaac. Val and Carolyn went on ahead to get seated, while Chris and Isaac went to the men's restroom. While Isaac was washing his hands, Calvin walked in the bathroom. He was surprised to see the little boy he had seen getting on the elevator and again sitting with the woman with the voice in his dream. Calvin went ahead and used the restroom. When he came out, he noticed that the little boy was still standing there, next to another young man as he washed his hands.

"Hello!" Calvin spoke to the boys.

"Hello!" Chris and Isaac said in unison.

"Hey, I have seen you before. Last year, when I and my father were here, we came to one of your classes. You had everyone laughing," said Chris.

"Yes, I do remember your face a little, and I do remember having everyone laughing," Calvin said.

"Ha-ha-ha-ha," they all laughed.

"And who might you be, young man?" Calvin asked Isaac.

"My name is Isaac. This is my first time coming here. I wanted to come, so my mom would not be by herself," Isaac responded.

"What a man you are! What is your mother's name?" said Calvin.

"Her name is Valoria, but her nickname is Val. Well, it was nice meeting you, mister, but we have to go." Isaac and Chris walked out of the bathroom in a hurry, as if they were late for something. Calvin went into the service on the opposite side from where Val was sitting. When the service was over, he and the party he came with decided to go out to eat at a restaurant outside of the hotel. While they were out, Calvin was very quiet. His friend asked him, kind of privately, while the other three were deep in a debate, "Calvin, what's up with you, man? You've been kind of distant minded since we have been here. What's bothering you?"

"Do you remember that dream I told you, about that woman's voice that I heard in my dream eleven months ago?" Calvin replied.

"Yes, what about it?"

"Well, Friday afternoon, when we were eating at the hotel restaurant, I heard that voice again."

"So, you are hearing voices now, ha-ha-ha-ha-ha."

"No, man, seriously, she is here at this convention. I heard a woman who was sitting right behind us say that exact statement, with that same voice," Calvin insisted.

"Man, are you serious?" At this time, they both did not notice that the other three friends had gotten quiet and begun to listen to what they were talking about.

"Yes, and what's funny is that I keep seeing her son, but I have not seen her yet."

"Do you even know her name? Maybe someone knows who she is."

"I saw her son in the bathroom tonight, and I asked him what her name was. He told me it is Valoria."

When he said her name, his friend's wife spoke up and said, "That is the new lady who held the woman's seminar this year. She is very intelligent. I really enjoyed her class. What about her?"

Calvin really did not want to tell anyone else why he was inquiring about her because he knew how women could be when they get new gossip. All of the women at his church and a few surrounding churches had already preyed on him. The last thing he wanted to do was cause uproar about his curiosity. "I just met her son and his friend in the bathroom. His friend recognized me from my class last year. He did not lie, but he kept it simple. His friend understood and knew what that was about, so he left it alone as well.

While Val was returning her rental car, Calvin was returning his on the opposite side of the airport. They both had to go up the escalator. Calvin finished before she did, so he headed up the escalator first. There was an older gentleman a few steps ahead of him holding an oxygen tank. When he got to the top of the stairs, the old man managed to pull one of his cords out of the tank, so Calvin stopped to help the man. When he was done, he reached down to grab his hand luggage, and exiting the escalator was Valoria and Isaac. When Calvin looked up, he saw the little boy with his mother, finally. It was the woman who got on the elevator at the hotel and whom he thought was beautiful. He looked down at her finger as she walked by to see if she was wearing a ring. His flight at that point was calling for boarding. Isaac looked at Calvin and waved. Valoria looked back to see who he was waving at. The most intriguing thing happened at that point. Val and Calvin made eye contact. Calvin was stunned by her beauty even more. And Val thought, *He is very handsome*. She gave him a friendly smile and continued walking.

"Isaac, why did you wave at that man? Do you know him?" Val asked her son.

"He was at the convention, Mom. We were in the bathroom, and he asked me what your name was." Val frowned with concern on why he would ask what her name was, and they had not even met yet. It was her first time seeing him. She looked back instantly. She noticed that he was still standing there, looking. When she looked back, he hurried into her direction. She stopped to let him catch up. She thought, if he was at the convention, he must know about my class and, perhaps, had a question or wanted to ask me something about the convention.

Calvin walked up to her and introduced himself. "Hello, Valoria, my name is Calvin. I saw you this weekend a few times, briefly, and wanted to introduce myself. I heard you taught a wonderful class."

"Well, thanks, I must say it was a good class, challenging, but it was good," Val replied. She was amazed to see how handsome he was. In fact, he was almost perfect. He was everything she desired in a man, physically. They called last call for boarding his flight.

"Well, it was nice meeting you, Valoria, and you, too, Mr. Isaac." Calvin turned to walk away and so did Val. Calvin turned back around again and called out, "Ms. Valoria?"

"Yes?" Val answered.

"Are you married?"

"No," she said.

Calvin smiled. "Well, maybe I'll talk to you later."

"Okay, maybe."

When Calvin returned to his home, he was kind of disappointed at himself that he did not ask for Val's number at the airport.

Calvin was determined to find her and make contact. He sat on his couch and thought about his first step. He then got excited; he picked up his phone and began to make some calls.

Val and Isaac had made it home. Val went to her room to unpack. While she was unpacking, she began to talk to the Lord out loud. "Lord, who was that man? Could he have been looking for me? Lord, please tell me why that handsome man was watching me like he already knew who I was. I have had many men approach me and flirt with me, but he just felt different. Lord, I don't understand. Why do I feel this way? I want someone in my life, but I am fine with being alone. Lord, please take these thoughts of that man out of my head. It just seems to be unreal how he had every physical aspect in a man that I want. I have never met or seen a man who was just what I wanted. I don't even want to think that, maybe, even though he was more than attractive to me, his mind is probably not right, or maybe his relationship with you is new. Who knows? Lord, please just take these negative thoughts out of my head. You have already healed me of my bitter thoughts and ways." That night when Val laid down, her mind was so clear. She did not have any dreams. She slept so peacefully.

Calvin, on the other hand, tossed and turned as if he slumbered while still had unfinished business.

It was a new day at the office, and Val was more than prepared. She came back to the office well-rested and excited to see how some of her clients were progressing. She went into her office and noticed that her voice mail light was blinking. So she pressed PLAY to hear the message, it was Charity. "I had to call and tell you before I forgot about it. I am out at the local steakhouse, and you won't believe who I saw sitting at the same table. I'm not gossiping, but I just wanted to tell you because I thought it would be some good news for you to hear. It's Allen and Leia was sitting by herself at first, and then Allen came in with another man and a woman who looked to be the man's wife or something. Allen also had the baby. He came over and spoke to me and brought the baby over to my table. Val, you would not believe, but the baby looks exactly like Antwan. It almost brought tears to my eyes. When he turned to walk away from my table, he noticed Leia sitting at the table alone, and he went over to show her the baby and talk to her. After sitting there for about fifteen minutes, he handed Leia the baby to hold, and he went back to the table with the couple he came in with to get the baby bag. I just thought it was beautiful for him to give her some company. I hope you are having a fun trip, and I'll talk to you later."

Business was going as normal. Val was seeing new people and updating existing clients. Four weeks had passed since she had gotten back from the convention. It was Tuesday morning when she came in the office and noticed that she had a card from Allen with a letter attached and a picture of the baby. The letter read:

Val,

I just wanted you to know that my life has taken a dramatic turn. The Lord has blessed me with a very special friend who I met in your office; you might know her as Leia I never thought that I would ever trust anyone ever again, but Val, it is so amazing how she is helping me with my grandbaby, and I did not even ask her for it. We just began to encourage each other and go to church together as friends. She is a very beautiful person. There had been times that I wanted to break down and come see you, and I know that I am always welcome, but you were right, Val, I have to carry my own cross. I am a man and a grandfather made father. I thank God that he has given me the strength to continue to press on. I'm starting to appreciate Leia more and more every day, and if the Lord wills it, this time next year, she will be my wife. Well, I just wanted to send you a picture of my son and give you an update on my life. I will stay in touch. God Bless.

Allen

Val had a 2:30 P.M. appointment with Charlene. When Charlene arrived, Val noticed that she had a distant look on her face. "Hello, Charlene, you look so distant today. Talk to me," Val said.
"I've been coming to you now for over a year, and I may have donated a total of 400 dollars, yet you still continue to treat me like I have given you thousands. Val, it's like when I leave from our visit, I feel fine, but after a few days pass, I'm back down again. I don't know what I am doing wrong. I pray every day, I go to church faithfully, and I try to do everything the right way, but I just have these trust issues that will not go away," Charlene replied.
"Charlene, let me ask you something. Do you trust yourself?"
"Of course, I do. I mean, how can I not trust myself? I didn't do anything to myself to not trust myself."

"I did not mean it like that," Val explained. "I'm just saying that you made the comment that when you leave here, you are just fine, but after a few days, you are back in your down mode. Its sounds like encouragement makes you feel better, and it even can last for days, but just as soon, it fades. Charlene, encouraging yourself will last a lifetime if you want it to, but before you can do that, you must know that you can trust your own advice and uplift. I'm not saying that you don't trust your choices, but I am saying that maybe, you are not giving yourself enough credit. Charlene, the worst enemy you could ever have is you. You yourself recognize that my encouragement is temporary, it only last for a few days, but I want you to try to encourage yourself. I want you to over exceed your own feelings about yourself and your situation. Even if you feel like you are giving yourself more credit than you deserve, give it to yourself anyway. You must do it every day, every minute, and every hour. Every time you feel yourself getting down, speak positive and happy things into your life. You have to try, Charlene. If you can, get your focus off trusting other people and redirect your focus on yourself. Trusting others is a privilege for you to enjoy the company of others. It's not needed to make it in life."

"You are right, and you make a valid point, but I don't know where to begin."

"There is no start to finish, Charlene. You just have to begin when you are ready to start feeling the change."

When Charlene left this time, she still had that distant look on her face. Val did not know what to think at this point. She knew that Charlene had to make the choice to change her situation. Unlike other therapists, she did not prescribe medication or diagnose her clients with symptoms because she knew that the only answer to every human problem was Jesus. Val began to think about Alonda. "Charity?" Val called out.

"Yes, Val?" Charity responded.

"Could you please call the mental hospital and schedule a visit for me to see Alonda McNeely?"

"Will do."

When Val arrived at the state mental institution, she prayed before she got out of her car. She was escorted to Alonda's room, where she was tied down to a chair because of her rages. When she entered Alonda's room, tears filled Val's eyes. Alonda looked worse than the last time she had seen her. Her eyes were open, and she was breathing on her own. She had the saddest look on her face—sadness that came from the soul. Val sat down in the chair next to her and held her hand. "Alonda? It's me, Val. I came to see how you were doing. Can you hear me? If so, then squeeze my hand," Val said. Val waited to see if she would respond, but she did not. Alonda just sat there with this blank look on her face. Beside her was a table with a schedule of medications that they give her routinely every day. When Val looked at the chart, she recognized some of the codes that they use to determine the doses. She grabbed her forehead in anger because she realized that they were giving her too much medication that her body was sure to become dependent on the drugs just to survive. It would also guarantee her stay in the mental hospital for the rest of her life. "Alonda, I know you can hear me because they would have told me if you were deaf. When I saw you the last time, I had no idea that you were here because I would have visited you a long time ago. I am and will always be a believer of miracles, as long as you are breathing. God can bring you out even at this state of mind, you are currently in. I have faith and believe that with all of my heart. Alonda, when other people speak to you, you may tune them out and allow the medication to numb your feelings, but as I am speaking to you right now, I know you are paying me full attention. If it's okay with you, I am going to pray for you, and I am going to pray for a miracle in your life, and when he brings you out, you will never give up on God again." As Val was speaking, she began to cry because the sympathy she felt for this woman was causing her to have extreme compassion. "Before I pray for you, I'm going to try to pull your mind out of that distant place that you are now in by putting happy memories in your head. The last time you came to my office, you were so happy because things had started going good for you. You just got a new job and you were on your way to buy a new car. You were so proud of your progress. I remember, right before you left my office, you asked me to pray with you. We prayed for about one hour. The spirit had gotten so high in my office. You began to shout in my office. When you were through praising him, you were so happy and filled with joy. No one could pay you millions to be sad or unhappy again." Val began to laugh a little, and then, she closed her eyes and began to pray, saying, "Lord, I'm coming to you on behalf of Alonda McNeely. Lord, she needs you more than she ever has. I don't know how she got to this point, Lord, but I am asking you for a miracle. I pray that she is praying with me at this very moment. Lord, she knows that you are the only one who can give her that peace and serenity she seeks. Lord, I know she would rather be at home praying and allowing you to work than to be here, a prisoner of man, diagnosed by their theories and calmed by their medication. Lord, I know everyone will not see that you are the only answer, but this woman knows. She has felt your presence. She knows how good it feels to praise you, even when things are not going well. No medication in the world can give her the peace that you can. Lord, please hear her cry for help. I'm speaking good into her life by faith. She will come out of this prison and praise you until her last breath." When Val finished praying, she opened her eyes and noticed that Alonda's eyes were closed. Val thought she had fallen asleep, so she grabbed her purse and was about to let go of her hand when Alonda squeezed her hand, opened her tear-filled eyes, and looked at Val. "Alonda? Can you speak to me?" Val asked. Alonda still did not speak because she was numb due to the medication. Val let go of her hand and stood up. "You may have given up the first time and stopped fighting, but you are still breathing, Alonda. Just trust him. Pick up your sword and let God fight for you through this, Alonda. You know what God can do. Don't give up again!" Val then walked out with tears in her eyes.

When Val arrived at work the next morning, she checked her email. She had received an email from the nonprofit organization business team. It was time for the annual meeting they held every year, to share ideas and get new information on running a nonprofit business.

The meeting was held at a nonprofit real-estate office, where they helped families find housing without having to pay closing cost or any other fees to purchase their own home. There was a total of sixty-five people this year at the meeting. It had actually expanded from the year before. Valoria was the only counselor (shrink) on that nonprofit business team. There was one lady, in particular, who stood out in the meeting because she came with a tablet full of questions, mainly asking about counseling centers that offered the same services as the ones that charge.

When the meeting was over and Val was about to leave, the woman approached her and said, "Hello, my name is Christina Ogle. I have been trying to find out where your office is located. I have heard nothing but great things about you and your services. I'm really interested in opening another nonprofit counseling center in the area. I have done my research and found that you would not lose out on your donations. Because we are nonprofit, our funding will always be secured," the woman said.

"I don't mind answering any questions you may have. I think it would be good for someone to open another office or two. As far as my funding is concerned, I will never worry because the only one who guarantees my income is God. I do not depend on the government or any other funding corporations to provide me with monies to run my business," Val replied.

"I understand, and wow, I see why you are so successful. You are very confident."

"Here is the address to my office and my direct line, so you can call me if you like."

"If you don't mind, I would like to come by and talk with you about this further."

"Okay, that will be fine," said Val. "Call me tomorrow, so I can clear a time for you to come by."

"Okay, thank you so much." When Val drove off, Christina thought about how she was going to tell Val who she really was.

Calvin had done his research and found out what state Val was in and her occupation. He decided to call her one morning at her office. It was Wednesday, at 10 A.M., and Val had just finished with a client. She was not expecting the phone call that she was about to get.

"Hello, this is Valoria," Val said.

"Well, hello, Ms. Valoria. I know you are probably wondering who this is," the man on the other end said.

"Yes, I would like to know who I am talking to," replied Val.

"This is Calvin Rucker. I'm the guy who introduced myself to you at the airport when we left the convention."

"Okay, I remember," Val said. "How are you doing?"

"I'm fine, and you?"

"I'm doing great," Val responded, then held the phone down and blushed as though she was a teenager getting her first call from a boy.

"Do you remember the last thing I said to you at the airport?"

"I sure do," she answered. "You said maybe you will talk to me later."

"Yes," Calvin said. "And the reason I said that was because I did not ask for your number. When I came home, I was determined to find you."

"And why were you determined to find me?"

"I can't tell you just yet. Don't worry. I'm not a psycho or anything. I am truly a man of God. I know I am calling you at your work, so I won't hold you long. I just wanted to tell you that I will be coming in town, where you live, in the next month and was wondering if I can take you to dinner."

"Well, I don't see why not," she said. "Why don't you take my cell number and just call me once you arrive?"

"Sure."

Val gave Calvin her cell number and spoke with him briefly after. When she hung up the phone, she was slightly puzzled why he was so determined to reach her. Since Val had been living for Christ, she did not question God. She let things go in the direction in which they were going because she knew that God would not allow anything to hinder her relationship with him.

It had been three weeks. There was one week left before Calvin was supposed to come in town, and today was the day another counseling center would be opening. Val promised Christina that she would come to her ribbon ceremony. Val was running a little late due to one of her clients' appointments going over. After the ribbon ceremony, Christina asked Val to go to lunch with her. Val decided to leave her car at the center and ride with Christina.

On the way to lunch, Christina had to stop by her condo. "Val, I hope you don't mind, but I have to stop by my house to pick up this form I need to drop off on the way back. This way, I won't have to backtrack. I also would like to change out of this suit and put on something more comfortable," Christina said. When they walked into Christina's house, Val was impressed by her style. "Would you like something to drink? Make yourself at home," Christina offered.

"No, thank you, I'll wait until we get to where we are going. I would not want to ruin my appetite," Val responded. When Christina ascended upstairs, Val sat on the sofa, and next to it was a picture frame that had a picture of Christina and her family. When she picked up the picture frame, a pamphlet of some sort fell out from behind the frame. As Val picked up the paper, she turned it over, and when she did, it startled her to see what it was. It was an obituary, the obituary of the little old lady with the purse who died and left her the money. Val stood up immediately, like she had seen a ghost.

By this time, Christina was coming back downstairs. Christina was saying something, but Val was so stunned to see the picture. She did not know what to say. "Val, what's wrong? You look like you just seen a ghost?" Christina said.

"Oh, no, it's not that," Val replied. Then Christina looked down and saw the obituary lying on the table.

"Val, I'm sorry," Christina said.

"Sorry for what?" Val asked.

"Can I talk to you about something while we are riding?"

"Sure."

"I am so sorry that I did not tell you earlier. I just did not know how to."

"Tell me what?" Val asked with an anxious and concerned look on her face.

"Right before my grandmother died, she called me and told me about this woman, and the good deed that she had done," answered Christina. "She told me about a time when she had the opportunity to do a good deed and how her selfishness interfered with making the best choice, and because of it, a woman and a child lost their lives. She told me when this woman did what she should have done, it caused her to regret every selfish decision she had ever made, and because of it, she was going to leave me most of her money. She told me to invest in a business to help people that would not cost them a penny. That day, my grandmother talked about you, Val. She cried and begged me to never turn anyone down who needed help. My grandmother told me that if she had the choice to choose one friend for me, it would be you. I did not mean to keep this from you, Val, but I had to meet you, the woman who inspired my grandmother to change her life right before she died. Val, my grandmother prayed to God to forgive her for all the wrong she had ever done. She spent the last two months of her life praying. Two weeks before she died, she had me pick her up for church so that she could be baptized." Val could not believe her ears. She had no idea that this woman made these choices before she died. "Val, you didn't even know my grandmother, but because of your good heart and your good works, you inspired the one woman I never thought could or would ever change, my grandmother." Christina became very emotionally upset. "Val, please forgive me. I don't want you to think I tried to deceive you because I didn't. I promise. I just did not know how to tell you."

"Christina, it's okay, really, but can I tell you something?"

"Anything."

"If we are going to be friends, you have to know that it is okay to talk to me," said Val.

They shared a laughed and went to lunch.

The time had come for Calvin to arrive in town. Val was out doing a little shopping when her phone rang.

"Well, hello, Ms. Valoria," Calvin said in the other line.

"Well, hello, Mr. Calvin," Val responded. Val had totally forgotten about the exact time he was supposed to come in town.

"Did I catch you at a bad time?"

"No, Sir, I'm just doing a little shopping," Val replied, smiling. She would always get the smiles for some reason when he called.

"So, do you think you will be free for dinner tonight?"

Val stopped in her tracks. "Are you here?"

"Yes, I am. I arrived this morning, but I had to take care of a few things first before I called you."

"What time do you have in mind for dinner?"

"How about 7:30, is that too late or early?"

"No, that would be perfect. Isaac will be going skating with some friends of his around that time, so that will be perfect."

"Okay, good, so I guess I will call you back around 6:00 P.M. to get directions so that I can come and pick you up."

"Okay, great."

When Val got off the phone, she headed straight home to find something to wear. Time had gone by fast. Val was looking out of the window, waiting for Calvin to pull up. As soon as she pulled the curtains back for the last time, he was pulling up. Val grabbed her purse and headed outside. When she walked around the bush in front of the front porch, she was surprised to see this tall handsome man standing by the passenger side door, waiting to open and close it for her.

"Just so you know, this is always," Calvin said.

Val looked at him and smiled as if saying, "Really?"

When they arrived at the restaurant, Calvin had already made reservations for a booth table by the window overlooking the lake.

"You seem to know your way around here," observed Val. "Are you familiar with this area?"

"Well, I have attended a few business meetings here, but I did not get out and sightsee," Calvin explained. "I am the type of man who does not ask too many questions. I'd much rather find it on my own. I printed off a map of the city, and from there, I can find my way. I'm really good with direction."

Val was very impressed. "That is so good to know. You strike me as a man who knows how to get what he wants."

"Not necessarily. I don't pursue my wants like you may think. I just follow my heart and go in the direction God leads me. Val, I know it may seem a little weird to you that I would make this trip just to see you, whom I barely know."

"Now, why would I think it's weird? That's how you get to know someone. You have to visit and talk from time to time. Besides, you did not make this trip just to see me." Val began to giggle. Calvin looked at her and smiled, then something dawned on Val, so she asked, "Calvin, did you make this trip just to see me?"

"Val, sometimes, when God tells us to do something, we should not question him," replied Calvin. "We should just move on what it is. That's why so many miss their blessing—because they doubt God and don't trust him. I have learned over the years that some things cannot be explained. We live in this world of unexplained situations. So, I learned to trust God and let the explanation come in the good result of obeying him. Val, I have been praying for something for some years now. I want to tell you about that something that I prayed for, and how he gave it to me. There was one point in my life that I thought that he was not listening to me. I thought that my prayer would never get answered. I had to ask the Lord to forgive me for doubting him and get back on track. I came here because I followed my heart. Val, I prayed and prayed, and God gave me an exact answer that was so clear, and I could not ignore it."

"I normally do not ask about someone's prayer, but I am so eager to know what it was. I love to hear about the goodness of God and the great things he does." There was no way Val could have prepared herself for what he was about to say.

"I prayed for a 'wife' Val. A faithful woman of God. A woman who loves him more than she does herself. A woman who puts God first in everything she does," he said.

"Are you getting married?" she asked.

"I hope so, if she accepts," Calvin answered. "That's why I came here: to get my wife—the woman who God led me to and confirmed to me, without even knowing her, what he was giving to me and only me."

"Who is she?" Val asked. When she asked that question, the comment he had made a few moments earlier had come to her mind, when she asked him if he was there to see her. He never really answered the question directly. "Who is she?"

"She is you! Val, I came here because you are my wife."

Val was shocked, so shocked, until she became utterly silent. During her silence, her mind began to replay all of the prayers that she could remember, and as they played, she was looking at him, noticing every detail. It was clear to her that this was the man she had described to the Lord. Every detail, down to his conversation, was what she had prayed for as well. It was like putting the last puzzle piece together in slow motion to complete the picture. She asked, "So are you? Right here? Right now?"

"Asking you to marry me?" replied Calvin. "Yes, I am. You are a stranger to me, Val, but not to God. He knows who you are and he knows who I am, and I am a strong believer that anything that God puts together, nothing in this world would be able to tear apart. I will not doubt God on this because he has showed me and been too good to me already."

Val looked at him with an unsure look, but she knew how God worked—in very mysterious ways. They both knew that people would think that they were crazy because they did not even really know one another. Val also knew that even though God worked in mysterious ways, he had not confirmed to her that this was her husband.

"Calvin, I don't know what to say at this time. Please do not be too disappointed," Val replied.

"I'm not, Val. I prayed that the Lord would let you know somehow that it is alright. I want you to take your time, and when he gives you conformation like he gave to me—and I know he will—I am already ready," he said.

While Calvin was taking Val home, he noticed that she was really silent. He felt that she might have been a little uncomfortable, so he kept his conversations very short and simple. He prayed in his mind and heart that he followed his heart and the direction God had led him to for certain. Calvin knew that God did not tell him the exact approach to make, but he was so excited and tired of waiting that he took it upon himself to just go and get her instead of waiting. Calvin knew that if God was giving her to him, there was no way she would say no. Calvin, typically, was very patient, but for some reason, his patience had worn thin. He began to pray that he did not move too fast, so fast that he would scare her away.

When Calvin dropped Val off, he opened the door again and walked her to her door. "Val, you have a beautiful night, like the woman you are," Calvin said.

"Thanks, Calvin, you do the same. How long are you in town for?" Val asked.

"I leave first thing in the morning."

"Will you call me before you leave?"

"I sure will. Oh, and before I forget..." Calvin reached in his pocket and pulled out a folded small piece of paper and handed it to Val.

"What's this?" When she looked up, he was walking away. She watched him get in his rental car and drive off before shutting the door. Val sat on the couch and took her time opening up the small piece of paper. As soon as she got it opened, she was in another state of shock. It was a beautiful diamond engagement ring on the inside of a picture of a lily, her favorite flower. She slipped on the ring, knowing that it would be either too small or too big, but the ring fit just perfectly. It puzzled her. How did he know her ring size without asking her? She had not worn a ring in years. She noticed the writing on the back of the small piece of paper. When she looked at it, it read: I asked God for my wife's ring size. I hope it fits. Val smiled, sat back in her chair, and stared at the ceiling.

That morning, right before Calvin was about to get on the plane, he called Val. "Hello, Val, it's me. I'm just calling to let you know that I am about to board the plane."

"Have a safe trip...and Calvin?" Val said hesitantly.

"Yes?" Calvin asked.

"That's what I was about to say..."

www.ingramcontent.com/pod-product-compliance
Lightning Source LLC
Chambersburg PA
CBHW021449070526
44577CB00002B/332